The Green Hill

The Green Hill

By

Richard Newman

... a story of Walton, a Yorkshire village

Published by lulu.com

Copyright © 2011, Richard Newman

Richard Newman has asserted his rights under the Copyright, Design and Patents Act 1988 to be identified as the author of this work.

First published in the United Kingdom by lulu.com

ISBN 978-1-4477-5726-9

Printed and bound in the United States by Lulu.com

This book is inspired by Jennifer Wormald whose persistence in ensuring that this story be told resulted in this chronicle.
Thank you, Jennifer, for leading me on a journey on which I am still travelling.

Other Books by the Author

'The Crown of Martyrdom' – a story of Ludwig van Beethoven and his letters to the 'Immortal Beloved.'

'The Horse that Screamed' – a tale set in the town of Guernica during the Spanish Civil War at the time of its destruction.

'The Potato Eaters' – set in Amsterdam in 1950, this is a story of madness and retribution set against a backdrop of collaborators attempting to leave Holland.

Thank you

Goes to Freda, and Nanette, and Bill and James and a host of others who gave me their stories, and to my wife Julia who eyed the manuscript with her usual candour and allowed me to come out the other side in one piece.

A Green Hill

Walton is one of those villages connected at either end by a lane looping back to a main road. As a result it has tended to remain in a time warp which most, if not all of its villagers prefer. Traffic passes as a low rumble behind the hedgerows and drivers may ponder idly at times on why the fields at the entrance to School Lane are so evenly ridged and furrowed.

The fact is Walton has sat on its green hill for a thousand years, give or take a few and even before this there is evidence of local tribes cashing in on its defence potential.

Like all towns and villages in England, Walton has received its fair share of pestilence, hunger, expansion and well-being. It has remained close-knit, as newspapers like to describe such places, mourning the loss of its shop and post office but enjoying the calls of the cricket teams behind and below the church. How many villagers even know that cricket, or a form of the game, was played out here in the 17th century?

This book sets out to paint pictures in your mind, told as *a* story (and not *the* story) rather than as a dry history volume. If there are errors, and I am sure locals will have differing interpretations on historical events, then please forgive me.

In the end, this is a very special village in a very special county – 'God's county' as the vicar of any time in the past would well have described it.

Richard Newman Boston Spa 2011

Chronology

Early years

c.45 A.D. Brigantes tribe had an enclosure in Waleston

c.180 A.D. Rudgate built from Aldborough to Adel

410 A.D. Romans left Britain for good

11th Century

1066 A.D. King Harold marches south from Stamford Bridge

1066 A.D. William Rufus (the Conqueror) kills Harold at Hastings

1086 A.D. Survey of Britain recorded in the Domesday Book; Waleston mentioned

12th Century

1143 A.D. Jueta de Arches marries Adam de Brus

1150 A.D. Grant made to Monkton Priory

1150 A.D. William de Arches dies

1154 - 1181 A.D. Chapel built in Waleston

13th Century

1206 A.D. Fairfax gives King John a palfrey

1220 A.D. York Minster begun

1225 A.D. Agreements made with Monkton Priory

1270 A.D. Market rights granted in Tadcaster

14th Century

1325-1350 A.D. New church built in Waleston

1348-1349A.D. Black Death arrives in the North

1349 A.D. Elizabeth de Elton marries Thomas Fairfax

1369 A.D. Burials and Baptisms permitted in Waleston

1378 A.D. Waleston declared to be a 'thriving place to live'

1393 A.D. John Fairfax buried below St. Peter's chancel floor

15th Century

1431 A.D. Joan of Arc burnt at the stake

1455 A.D. War of the Roses begins.

1461 A.D. Battle of Towton

1464 A.D. Yorkists defeat Lancastrians at Hexham

1470 A.D. York Minster completed

1486 A.D. War of the Roses ends. Henry VII marries Elizabeth of York

1495 A.D. Thomas Fairfax made a Knight

16th Century

1536 A.D. Reformation. Smaller monasteries dissolved first

1536 A.D. Monkton tithes now sent to Lord Latymer and Walton

1538 A.D. Plague returns to the village

1574 A.D. Thomas Ripley is given a curacy for life

1598 A.D. Parsonage in Walton willed to Julyan Snawsell

1598 A.D. Tithe barn in Walton mentioned by Oswald Chambers, Rector

17th Century

1611 A.D. St. James's bible published

1642-1649 A.D. Civil War breaks out. Wetherby occupied by Parliamentarians

1644 A.D. Battle of Marston Moor. Sir Thomas Fairfax involved

1645 A.D. Battle of Naseby. Sir Thomas Fairfax involved

1696 A.D. Window tax

18th Century

1743 A.D. Curate unable to live in vicarage as it is in ruins

1756 A.D. Village shop in Walton.

1786 A.D. First mail coach to Wetherby

1779 A.D. Captain Cook killed in Hawaii. News in Walton prob. 1780

1788 A.D. Insanity of George III

19th Century

1805 A.D. Battle of Trafalgar. Admiral Lord Nelson dies

1847 A.D. School built in Walton

1861 A.D. George Lane-Fox offers to buy land for the church. Problems arise

1887 A.D. Queen Victoria's golden jubilee

1890 A.D. Faculty granted of £1,100. Salisbury is Prime Minister. Church closes

1891 A.D. Walton church reopens

20th Century

1914 A.D. WWI breaks out. Kitchener's appeal

1915 A.D. Coalition Government

1918 A.D. Rationing introduced

1939 A.D. WWII breaks out
1941 A.D. Royal Ordnance factory set up
1943 A.D. Lionel Griffith sets up shop
1977 A.D. James Scott arrives as last of the line
2011 A.D. Bill Kilby rings the bells at St. Peter's

Contents

Foreword

It is on a steep grassy bank that Walton church sits, its strong reinforced foundations built to take the thrust of its tower upon the slope. Like that other green hill far away, it seems to its parishioners as if it has been there forever.

There *has* been a building on the top of this terminal moraine, a left over from a former ice-age, for as long as time brought man to this area, firstly for defence reasons and later because it enabled him perhaps, to feel closer to God.

This is a story, a story of one church and its village, for centuries so intertwined that it is impossible to separate the two from each other, bonded like Siamese twins.

It is only now, in the twenty-first century that the fabric is beginning to unravel as '*residents*' leave for work in the cities in the early morning and return late in the evening. During the day their houses often stand silent and empty, their owners ignoring, as we all seem to do, the seasons, and the weakening bonds of the ageing residents whose ready offers of help to solve the problems that this Kingdom imposes upon them are all too often forgotten in the mad dash for modernism. And secularism, once again popular, reduces the number of worshippers to St. Peter's as surely as the Black Death achieved over six hundred years earlier.

Walton or *Waleston* as it was once known slumbers now in the summer sun as I write, enjoying its fêtes and strawberry teas and cricket matches as it always has, but there are few interested to learn of the days when the Romans possibly used the high point as a signalling station, or the sale of most of the hamlet to just one man. There's the arrival of the Plague, and its dreadful return more than once, the War of the Roses in between and the horror of the Civil War, one such battle of which took place just a couple of leagues away.

As the village grew, there were plans to merge with adjoining villages; there came a need to spread the parson and the curate more thinly as he was asked to preach in other local churches as well as his own and the voices from London often dictated what the people could or should worship. Sounds familiar?

Today the village street is lined with the enamelled plinths of cars; before, it was the cart and the horse which blocked the road and even earlier it was potholes in a difficult rutted track to walk on which led up to the Chapel or down to the Great Hall where the Manorial Lord lived. Family names remain, some familiar such as the Lane-Fox's and the Fairfax's, but the de Arches once owned Waleston as we would own a rather comfortable cottage in the Lakes, just as Wetherby was sold by the Sixth Duke William Cavendish to fund his plans for Chatsworth.

Walton provided a living for many people through the centuries from the Squire and the Reeve, the serf and the vassal and to Jacob Clough who ran the shop and dealt with funerals and the law, the sale of property, arranged the marriages, all within his busy day in the shop which would sell just about anything you needed.

Like any other village or town throughout the years, the village suffered and enjoyed poverty and plenty in more or less equal measures affected early on to quite some degree by the enormous building programme which continued for over two hundred and fifty years in York. Imagine building a cathedral today and being told it would be finished in 2261 A.D?

When a visitor arrives in the village he or she will notice the ridges and furrows of the pasture alongside the main road the evidence of long-dead farmers; when one flies over it, the mediaeval fields can still be clearly seen running down the hill away from the church. If Jacob Clough was to return and climb the church tower today he would see much he would have recognised in the days when his shop catered to such a wide range of services. Now, the shop is gone; the post office has succumbed to external pressures and the lonely bus stop signifies the only method of travel to Wetherby if one is not a car owner.

What is certain in this shifting story of a small corner of England is that when we have all finally shuffled off this mortal coil, the green hill and the church will still be there.

Chapter One

Mists, Fog and Early Days

William d'Arques leaned back in his chair, the better to stare into the blazing fire while at the same time not to burn his face. His wife, Beatrice, gazed at him expectantly waiting for the answer to her question. "What was on the hill? I mean, before we came here? And the village, has it always been here?"

The truth was, he did not know, though he had been told stories by some of the older men in the huddle of wattle and daub huts they called a village, the stories often conflicted with each other. He had had to translate from the mixture of tongues they used, mainly German but a form of Danish as well; whatever, it came from across the seas east of York.

"Once, there were clever people from another land, much farther away than where the Angles came from. Tough, fighting men, with good armour and a discipline we rarely see today. I am told they built the road through Rudgate."

"So, we did not build it then?"

"No, no. We do not have the knowledge or the skills to do this, although old Leif repairs some of the worst holes. One day it will wear out and then we will be forced to go back to the ruts and holes as we have here in the village."

"And after them, what then?"

William stirred and looked at his wife. He sighed to himself. Beatrice had always been the clever one, always seeking new knowledge and novel, easier ways of trying to do the same thing. "A small wood chapel, then later, stone perhaps. Two hundred years ago the local people would have needed some where to pray, to shelter, to be nearer to God. Then, William the Bastard came and we came too. We dealt with their king, Harold, and began the building programme. That is when William gave us these lands. This is what I do know."

Beatrice smiled to herself watching her husband assert himself as he must in front of the servants. "One day we need to build a church here on top of the hill."

"One day, yes. At the moment I have the more pressing need to alter my name. These locals, with their queer tongue keep getting my name wrong. I've beaten a few of them but still they call it 'Arcs.' Perhaps if I saw to change it to, say, 'Arcs?'"

"Or Arches. De Arches perhaps," interrupted Beatrice." From Arches, it will tell the people where you came from."

"Hmm, maybe. Even if our son was born in Arques he is growing up here and will probably remain here all of his life. Perhaps we could give our name to the village so he will not forget it."

"Osbern will be a fine man and I trust if he is blessed with children that a son can be named after you." The fire crackled with comforting warmth as they both contemplated the idea.

"By the way, Our Lord King William is planning to make a register, a complete list of every piece of land, every carucate, every plough and cow-"

"For what reason?"

"I was about to tell you, my dear," William replied quite accustomed to his wife's interruptions. "To see if he is receiving all of the taxes he needs. This building is expensive."

"It is, if it is on the scale of York."

William, or Guillaume d'Arques had been born in Arques in Northern France and had married Beatrice de Bolbec in 1055 A.D. William was probably the first whose arrival in Walton was sufficiently important to record the event. Fighting alongside his namesake, William the Conqueror, the grateful victor had rewarded his knight with rich and fertile lands in the north where he brought his wife and son to live down by the river. It was a fairly hard existence in those days though in comparison with the local population it was perhaps considerably more comfortable. The coming of the Domesday record focussed many a mind on what taxes needed to be levied in the future and whether, now under the burden of the French, they would turn out to be harsh task-masters. Waleston, as it was known locally even with its tiny population, would not be missed off from the register and, as it turned out, it was becoming recognised as a village of some substance.

While modest Waleston progressed, mighty York began to suck in a huge amount of energy and funds, making the surrounding villages wonder if it was ever going to stop. It was one thing to give to the glory of God, they would grumble, it was entirely another when their own village got very little at all. Meanwhile, the abbeys and monasteries, along with the monks grew fat and shiny as they sold their religious relics, which had no credibility at all. But, in days without communications except by word of mouth, such wonders as a splinter from *the* Cross would amaze and fascinate the locals who had no other basis to believe other than what they were told by the men of the cloth.

Beatrice did not live to see the prophecy come true but within sixty years of her death, York's demands for money, labour and materials, especially stone and carved stone had begun to tell. Masons became in short supply and the villages began to suffer.

It was Jueta, Beatrice's granddaughter, who began to sense the tensions in the air. Even at fourteen years old she saw there was a pressing need for Waleston to have, at the very least, a chapel on the hill where an enclosure had stood in the centuries before. After all, T'orp Arches had a church and had had one before the Great Register fifty-four years earlier before she had been born.

But William, her father, had also seen the problem. Ailing, his final wish was to ensure that Waleston got its chapel 'in the Norman style,' he had demanded. His failing eyes alighted on his shield above the fireplace with its three silver arches.

"My mother foresaw we would build a chapel. It is as if this hill was created by God to carry one of his churches. One day perhaps, my children's children will see a church here in Waleston." And almost as if he was in tandem with his wishes, his eyes closed for the last time as the foundations were driven deep into the ground.

Jueta knew the building would turn out to be a much more complex matter. Her father had provided the funds to Monkton Priory and installed Matilda, his second daughter as prioress. Money also had gone to Hammerton in the east causing, inevitably, arguments every time funds were required. Matilda learnt quickly to hold on to her money and to conduct her business with an iron will and ignored the cries of "it isn't fair on us."

Over the polish of her desk she focussed on two feet, which as she raised her eyes to the face, began to shuffle uncomfortably. "This chapel, this chancel in Waleston. It is taking far too long to build and it is taking too much of my, our money, here in Monkton. Surely the people in that village can provide more labour?"

"But, Reverend Mother, they are already giving three days a week to his Lordship's fields and another two to their own crops-"

"That leaves two does it not? Besides, they get almost eight weeks a year holiday."

"One day is the Lord's day, Prioress. Surely-"

She cut him off again sharply, not liking to be lectured on something she already knew. She banged her fist on the oak top making both men in front of her, jump. "Never mind," she answered irritably, "we shall just have to take more from Hammerton. And, mind you see these people from Waleston don't shirk when they do turn up. I want this running sore off the Prior as soon as possible. Understood? It's been...what?"

"Five years Prioress. Another two harvests and we should be able to consecrate the building." The second of the men whose hat had been ground between his hands as he wiped the sweat off his palms was only too keen to get out of the door.

"And York," she threw after their retreating backs, "when will we ever see the end of that one?"

But they couldn't answer as they had no idea. The whispers in the countryside about a Cathedral, so tall that the Bishop would be able to step straight into God's Kingdom from the spire, were growing. It was, said witnesses, as if the stone pinnacles formed a protective wall around heaven itself.

Matilda waved the men away as if they had been flies on a jackass's nose, well aware that her image of supposed piety and conciliation were stretched as thin as a hair on Jack's horse for hire. Her problem was, she knew, that Waleston deserved something better. The village was growing in stature and there were important voices of dissent demanding better things in return for all the tithes they gave; ten percent of their output was lost from each man. There had to be a return. She was well aware that an original grant from Adam de Brus for the benefit of the village had been transferred to Archbishop Roger's new foundation in York and would inevitable cause problems in the future.

Matilda sighed again allowing her gaunt, deeply etched face to soften for a moment. Her original wish in life to serve God in a simple way and remain in obscurity had gone with the daily grime of the Priory church politics though united with the need to maintain strong diplomatic relations with the powerful land owners of the north had become her daily penance. Not for her a quiet seat in the sun with a passage from St. John to tax her clever mind. She sighed again and rose to prepare for Compline.

And, of course, dissention grew as surely as the oak tree on the corner of the road. It grew in direct proportion to the expenditure on the enormous Mynster as it was known. It was as if the sun rose and set on York while the villages surrounding the town remained in permanent shadow. It was all to do with 'Rights,' "...respective rights" as one member of the Council in Waleston put it.

It was a cold morning in March that a meeting was held in the Convent of Monkton. Representatives from T'orp Arches and Waleston made the eighteen mile journey in two carts, stopping the night in Hammerton before arriving, dust covered and hungry in the Visitors Hall. When they heard that Archbishop de Gray and his sacristan had also come personally, there were feelings of trepidation seeing now just what they had stirred up for it had become a hornet's nest and hornets honey was too dangerous to collect by normal means. Their petty grievances had risen far higher up the ladder than they could ever have imagined and at the moment they were expected to justify their actions as to why they had caused so much grief.

The Prioress arrived, followed by several postulants bearing food of simple but welcome fare accompanied with a large pitcher of cider. The men looked gratefully at the nuns who masked any feelings other than that of sanctity behind their coifs.

The meeting was brought to order by the sacristan, Master Gilbert. Following a quick prayer which Matilda felt was far too brief and uttered without any due feeling to the Latin words, he started off.

"My Lord Archbishop, Prioress, gentlemen. My Lord has convened this meeting to resolve, once and for all the arrangements currently in place between the Nunnery here in Monkton, the Chapel of Waleston and the Chapel of St. Mary and the Holy Angels in York. We propose," at this point, the sacristan's eyes roved around the expectant faces daring anyone to challenge his Archbishop's proposal, "we propose that the nuns of Monkton shall have the chapel of Waleston and all tithes and incidental fees pertaining," he paused again for effect but received a glare from his Archbishop to get on with it, "and one toft adjoining the chapel. They will receive also, one carucate of land in T'orp Arches as well as tithes of milk, wool, calves, pigs and any other tithes of cattle..." he paused, this time for breath. Matilda's eyes urged him on again, "and eight tofts in the town except a particular piece of land which remains....in my own mansion." The men eased their buttocks on the hard bench not wishing to challenge any of the edicts.

Matilda glowed with satisfaction. Let the man have his bit of land, it was a small price to pay. She knew that her firm stand from the beginning had been the answer to the pressure from all the men. Gilbert was droning on.

"We, in York, cede any and all rights in Waleston." The members from Waleston who had been listening carefully to the semi-legal language realised they had just lost one master and gained another, or rather, a mistress. But, just maybe, Monkton Nunnery would not be as demanding as York.

The Archbishop, who had until now been studying the nuns bent over in the gardens stirred in his chair. "You do realise, brethren, that all of your noise and disturbance to the natural peace and quiet of this corner of England has reached the ears of His Holiness, the Pope?"

Matilda was thunderstruck. The men of Waleston's mouths dropped open in unison as if they were about to sing in their choir, or more likely to be strung up over a fire.

"But, His Holiness is many leagues away from us. How did he hear-?"

"He hears everything, Reverend Mother, just as God sees everything and he was displeased with the dissention. However, he also realised there was some, I stress the word, *some* justification in the case you pleaded and thus His Holiness has graciously approved the changes. Thus, in effect, this grant is from Rome itself." The Archbishop warmed to his theme. "Change, great change is coming to Waleston. William Fairfax, who endeared himself to our late departed King John when he presented him with a palfrey, has bought Waleston from Peter de Brus."

"Yes, my Lord. Nine ox-gangs, one acre and three perches of land with the tofts and crofts included."

"You are indeed, Reverend Mother, well informed. News travels fast these days."

Master Gilbert smiled, dripping oil. That would end any further dissention once and for all. No-one went against the word of His Holiness. The men made their farewells and climbed back in the carts making their way down the track as charcoal burning smoke filled the valley. With luck they would be back home before nightfall. The Prioress, having entertained the Archbishop to a meagre meal of cold chicken and some overcooked perch and more cider, much to his disappointment, climbed into his saddle with Master Gilbert and several clerics alongside. He too would need to stop over away from the woods where too many people these days were only too keen to relieve them of a groat or two.

With clarity restored came hope and plans. More funds came from the tithes; seeds began to germinate, not only in the ground but in the Prioress's mind. As the village she administered grew, the chapel proved to be not nearly large enough for the swelling population freed of their fields for the day. What was needed was a church, a church with a tower high enough to be seen from across the river and beyond to York. In short a substantial building.

Aye, thought one villager; Waleston was going somewhere and a proper church was needed.

Chapter Two

A Door for the Devil

"We'd keep the east face of the tower then?" enquired one elder hunched in his fleecy cloak around a fire which lit the circle of faces, all freemen, with orange and yellow light. Smoke swirled behind them seeking an outlet. Gaunt faces these; the result of the poor harvest captured the shadows too easily, emphasizing the hardship and the urgent need to get the church plans agreed.

"And strong foundations, Jethro. The bank to the north is steep."

"We'll need a door for the devil...to flee the font," said another. "On the north side so he will fall down the hill in his haste." He giggled then, realising what he had said, and looked nervously back into the shadows. Lucifer was not a word one conjured with at will.

"But remember brother, we have no rights for burials or baptisms. These rights remain with T'orp Arch."

"But we may, one day receive those rights, so to put a door in now will save the expense later." Jethro, the builder, a small, powerfully built man with a lame leg dressed in clothes as dusty as a miller thought the idea of having a door just to allow Satan to escape when a child was baptised was an over-indulgence in a small church, but he held his peace. It would be extra work. He spoke instead of the windows. Pulling a length of charcoal from a pocket he drew a perfect pointed arch and divided it into reticulated tracery sections almost as if a spider had traced its body in ink.

"Tadcaster stone. Soft enough to cut such an arch. I have two good journeymen and I as a Master mason will do all of the supervision.

"But, the cost," interrupted another ignoring the self-importance oozing from the builder.

"Well, we could build square headed windows to the nave."

"Square headed? Square headed? What does that mean?"

"Flat, you dumpkin," said his friend Robert, not unkindly. It was all a case of keeping calm while the plan unfurled like a flag.

"And leave out the porch. That's money wasted at this time. Reduce the height of the tower but keep the foundations strong so you can make it taller at anytime in the future, God willing...or when we have the money."

The builder, Jethro added in an important afterthought; well, to him anyway. "We'll leave Osbern's arch to the existing tower. It will never fall down and built to last forever so it will cost a great deal to remove it. And for why? To leave it will look nice at the west end."

Jethro's clients, also his friends, became more and more excited. Mead and cider was called for and the fire was built up.

"If we cannot afford a large church, maybe we build in a low window...perhaps on the south wall...near the chancel arch, or a small doorway so that those in the fields who cannot come to church, perforce obliged to be working for our Lord Master, will know the service is beginning with the first words of the Sanctus."

"Good idea, brother," Jethro nodded his head approvingly. "So," he added by way of summary, "you need a church with a nave of about three rods in length and one and a quarter rods in width. You will retain the lower part of the tower as it exists together with its door and you want a fine window at the east end of the chancel."

"How much, Jethro?"

The builder scratched his head in time honoured fashion. "I can't just go an' give you a price like that. 'Ow much sand, 'ow much lime, the amount of cut stone? Journeyman's wages. My small amount. 'Ow much free labour is you goin' to give me, eh?"

"Just some idea, Jethro. So we can give this to the Convent of St. Mary. It is they who will give us the munificence after all."

"Well, nothin' short 'o two hundred and fifty nobles."

There was, to put it mildly a pregnant pause. "Praise be," said one, "that it should cost so much to worship God."

"It's up to you...and St. Mary's. I'll work out a fair price for the stone, the lime, timber. You let me know how many men will give something of their time."

"But, most already have to give time to the Manor. It leaves little time enough for their own land and as you well know it has been a very poor harvest last year."

"It will never be easy building a church, brothers. We have a poor harvest every four years or so and it is your plan, not mine."

Robert tapped his purse lugubriously. "That'll take a great many groats."

"About," the quiet man, much older than his brethren was attempting to multiply on his fingers. He gave up and snatched the piece of charcoal from the builder. He made copious scribbles. "It will take five thousand groats near as God makes it," he declared.

A groat was understandable. It was four pennies. Anything higher was not in the realms of everyday thought simply because no-one earned a noble, not that anyone had seen one and it was rumoured they were almost impossible to find. A half-noble was used at the Manor.

The quiet man, Peter, stood up, immediately stilling the gabble of voices. His age was respected.

"Brothers, as our good neighbour Jethro has said, no-one said it was going to be easy but with funds pledged from St. Mary's in York we can make a start."

There were grunts of approval. A village with a church, not a chapel was the difference between eating roast beef or venison rather than a mess of pottage. It was a good thing to dwell upon as the snow piled up against your toft wall and the grain store dropped towards the dusty floor until the stone flags showed through.

"So, Robert, we go and see the Reeve, and then with his blessing we'll make the journey to York."

"We will need help in the fields. Two days away, again-"

"Don't worry," said the elder with his fleece now tight about him as he prepared to go outside. "The village will work together especially if they know we are to have a church of our own. They will work the land for the Manor. Now we have an elected Reeve of our own he will see to our needs. Besides, he will want to be part of the great project himself."

"Our Master himself will take an interest. Book his space early, so to speak in the front row." He smiled at his small joke. The idea that the Lord of the Manor might be ousted from the front space in the nave was a joke to be shared.

*   *   *   *   *

The young wheat was colouring the fields with the lightest of green tinges when Robert, stretching his back as he tilled a patch of vegetables in his own ground, saw a horseman riding up the road past the chapel. The man was a cleric by his clothes but his horse was fit and well groomed and the man's boots were of expensive leather. Dust cloaked him from a long journey as he glanced up keenly at the small if strongly built chapel where it sat, defiantly overlooking the fields. He could see the Norman influence on the tower and the protruding, massive foundations, fit to take something much larger, he realised. He drew his horse up and Robert ran forward with a leather bucket of water which the animal sucked at greedily through his teeth.

"Master Robert?"

"Aye, I am he?" He smoothed his tunic down as he heard the educated voice.

"My name is Joshua and I come from York, St. Mary's and the Holy Angels to be precise."

"God bless you Sire. You have news?"

"Indeed I do," said the other smiling as he climbed down stiffly to shake hands. "You have your grant and you may proceed with the building."

Robert's wife was coming out of a hen coop as she heard the news. She shrieked with joy. "Robert. We will have a stone cut to mark the start. In the Year of Our Lord, thirteen twenty-five."

"Anno Domini," he added, laughing in delight.

"We shall have to find somewhere to worship while we take the chapel down," she responded with practicality.

"A barn will do. Somewhere out of the rain is all we need." Robert turned to the cleric and patted him on the back. "Come and have supper with us Sir. I would like you to meet with the elders of the village and our Reeve, Thomas is his name, a good-"

"And honest man. A serious but good fellow I think. We know of him and you could do worse than ask him to run the accounts for the building works. And, remember, you still need to find the rest of the money."

"We reckon, Sir, that with hard work it will take twenty-five years to complete."

"A morsel compared with York." Joshua said as he scratched his bald head and ran his fingers through a greying tonsure. "You, Brother Robert will be in a happier place by then is my reckoning."

"Aye Sir, but I shall be joyful anyway that we few here will have begun such a project which will last forever."

"Or at least, until Armageddon."

"Perhaps, even beyond. The builders here build strong. They know how to distribute the loads from the tower which is necessary."

"King William's foundations I see. And you are to retain part of the tower, excellent. This church is a living being carrying history along in its stones."

"There are stories here of times long past of a tribe known as the Brigantes who built an enclosure on this land. There are signs, everywhere. Then those men who came from the south, another land, who built the road hereabouts."

"Aye Robert. They were called Romans and they came from Rome, where our Holy Father lives. They left deep marks in York. Even in our new Minster under the south transept. We are building, now, on their foundations. Build like the Romans, Robert and your church *will* last forever."

Robert was fascinated with the story. He had often tried to guess the origin of the old track where ploughs sometimes pulled up dressed stones, some with deep wheel grooves. "Come and take a drink while I summon the village. Ruth, put the cow out for a while to make some space. You will stay the night Master Joshua and take a bowl of pottage with us? And some fine cheese."

"I will that, Robert. My horse will not travel on tonight. Besides, the forest at Wighill is fearsome as evening comes."

"Then you must best stay with us. We will draw some cider and talk of this great project in York. We all hear that the foundations are now cut."

Chapter Three

The Devil's Breath

And Robert was proven right. It did take twenty-five years to build the church and the tower. A decision had been made to leave out the weather porch for the time being, though in all other respects the church was completed long after Robert and his wife had passed on to a higher plane. But, before the lead dressings were in place, hammered down with hardwood bolsters, a black evil was advancing across the land leaving death and a dreadful helplessness in its wake.

The whole week, previously had been warm, a late spring, and now the blankets were being hung out to rid them of the winter's dampness and mildew. People stopped to chatter and gaze up at their church in the last stages of completion. So long had it taken to build that the winters' rains and frosts had already begun to soften the harsh grooves of the masons' chisels. Here and there, lower down where the stone had been exposed the longest, small orange and green marks of lichen had taken up a permanent anchorage.

Thomas, the Priest gloried in the day soon to come when he would see St. Peter's consecrated. He needed cheer after the depressing news of a woman in France, more of a maid, with her age being only nineteen, who had been burnt at the stake for heresy having been sold to the English for trial. There was something fundamentally wrong of the church to have allowed such a dreadful death, he knew, but it was the way of the world and once the court proceedings had started there was little anyone could do.

It was on this Monday morning that the world turned upside-down and all because of one surly youth. Thomas had risen to the cockerel at the fifth hour of the day; each day earlier as together they both gloried in the spring dawn. The sky was tinged with red, a shepherd's warning if ever there was and mackerel clouds spattered the heavens resembling pottage thrown from a giant's spoon.

St. Peter's sparkled in the sunshine, it's newly cut stone golden, just as some pilgrims described it, as Jerusalem is coloured. The small but fine church sat atop the highest hill in the village, a church at last, and no longer a chapel.

A knock at the door had brought an urgent summons from one of Ben's daughter's. Ben was the farmer whose byres nestled against the church's west boundary wall and who had given much of his time when the decision had been made for the rebuilding.

One of the rooms in the farm had been converted to a beer parlour where he sold mead and strong ale, and it was Molly, who served the drinks, who had been taken ill, "...desprit' ill, Sir" as Ruth had put it to the Priest. Yesterday in church the maid had seemed bright enough as he had said goodbye to her where she had stood looking up with wide eyes alongside Ben Smyth and his large family.

He hastened from his house having only half partaken of breakfast consisting of some left-over hare pie. As it was only a footfall or two, he arrived still chewing crusts of pastry which he quickly swallowed and thanked Ruth and shook hands with Ben whose frightened face was a world away from when he had last seen him at the south door of St. Peter's a day earlier.

"Father, come in, come in."

In the parlour, Mary his wife and his six children stood huddled together, some weeping.

"What on God's name is the matter with you all?" Thomas asked, appalled at the sight of so much misery. "How is Molly?"

"Molly's gone to her Maker, Father," replied Mary, bobbing towards him. "Molly died a few minutes ago."

The priest crossed himself quickly. "But, this cannot be. How could she have died so quickly? And of what?"

This statement set off new misery. "Please, Father, follow me."

The two men walked through the back door and into a yard leading to a small lean-to dwelling set in the side of the byre. "She's lying in there, Father." On entering he noticed that none of the family would follow, making him frown with unease.

Inside it was dark, there being no light of any kind, and dank. The strong odour of manure rose as it tried, unsuccessfully to blank out the smell of rotten decay. The stench was so disgusting that it took all of God's strength for him to lift the sacking thrown over the maid's face. He moved away from the doorway to bring some light to the face.

Urgently he backed out of the room and gave a sharp command, one that allowed no-one to disobey his word. "Lock this door Ben and let no-one in until I give you an order to do so. And keep the children well away from here."

"Is it-?" Ben clenched his hands together as he choked on his fear.

"At this time we do not know. At least Molly is at peace and in a better world. When did she become ill?"

"Yesterday... at Sunday lunch, Father. Molly did not want her meal and asked to lie down. We thought she had a drop of the palsy. But, there is a friar in York who says such illness comes from lead in the water. Now this..."

"You must keep calm, Ben. Your family will need you to be clear-headed...and tell no-one. I am going to the Hall."

The Great Hall was but three hundred yards away down the main street. Thomas walked quickly up the track where he could

see his Lord rotating a lure as he called to Jack his favourite
Peregrine to its meal.

"Good morning Father, what brings you so early?"

He was cut off rather rudely but there was little time for
niceties. "It's here, it's come, the devil's work itself."

"What are you talking about Father?" He stopped then and
shook a finger at the Priest. "The Great Pestilence?"

There was absolute silence; even the croak of frogs in the
fish pond seemed to lessen. "Are you sure?"

"Positive. Molly the maid... at Ben's... she's dead."

"Little Molly? But, yesterday in church."

"Yes, I know, it was that quick. Please hasten Sire. We
must summon the Parish Council. Can we meet here, and bring
the others quietly?"

Half an hour later six men sat around the table which had
been cleared of boots, dead rabbits, and a brace of ducks. The
mood was sombre, as if a funeral was under way. There was no
attempt to greet and shake hands. Grey, lined faces, more used
to dealing with a serious fire or a flood now had to deal with
something entirely new in their community. There could be no
help from any other village, or from York itself.

Their fathers could recall the terrible days thirty-five years
earlier when the marauding Scots had swept down from the
hills, almost savages in their frenzy, and exceptionally skilled in
the art of killing. They had, at last, withdrawn to their own lands
but this time death would be quite different. Death would come
as silent as a dove sitting on its nest, without any warning and
with no discrimination between young and old, women, youths
and those just starting life.

"What's to be done," asked the retired Reeve. His powers
of leadership had long gone and his rheumy eyes were already
staring death in the face.

Thomas answered for them all. "Molly must be removed
tonight and buried outside the village. Somewhere deep and
where the ground water will not be able to seep back into the

well." There was a murmur of agreement. There came a sudden knock at the door followed by a servant entering unbidden. His Lordship looked up in annoyance at being disturbed but took the message.

He paused as he read the crudely written note, then sighed and handed it to over. "It has broken out already. Ben's wife and two of the children have gone down with it."

"They must not be allowed to move outside their house," interjected a white-faced man with a scrawny beard and ferrety eyes which darted around the room as he sought approval. "The door must be nailed up."

"But food?"

"Food can be thrown over the wall. In a sack." Again came nods of agreement.

"It's too late." A hoarse voice, a sound which was cracked with fear, from the sixth elder who had been sitting in silence, listening to the discussion rose over the others. "I very much fear Satan is sitting on my knee."

He was a fit, tanned farmer in his late fifties. "Yesterday, I met Molly before church. We were both picking mushrooms and I helped her load her basket before she went off to change for service."

"Did you touch her, John?"

"Yes, Father. I shook her hand in farewell."

"Then there's no hope John. We are all dead men in here. In York, one man, woman or child is dying in every three and they say it is getting worse." The other men were appalled. "But that means...?"

"It means there could be seventy deaths in Waleston alone."

One by one the men rose, quickly anxious to be away, as none could look another in the eye. There were now more important things to deal with such as their wives and children.

"It's God's will," offered Thomas.

"Difficult to understand how an all-loving God would need to kill one in three of his children, and in such a manner," replied the noble. He patted the heads of two of his hunting dogs as if in farewell to his beloved animals.

No words of comfort would suffice, so, the Priest merely walked out into the brilliant sunlight which caught the luminous plumage of a jay flying across his path...and to the left; the second bad omen of the day.

In a field close to the path a youth of about twenty years was cutting a ditch to drain his Lord's land. Jed was a powerfully built lad like his father John. His surly character would never allow him a chance to become a freeman and he knew he would remain a serf all his life. He gave a curmudgeonly nod of his head to the men as they passed by. His father walked up to him.

"Jed. We are going to need a deep trench and you may have to make it bigger as time goes by."

His son gazed across the field. "So, it's come then? Like the devil's breath... from York?" His father nodded.

Thomas picked up the shaped turf spade he had been using to build the ditch. "Best get started then. Past the five acre...perhaps in Fox's Wood?"

"Aye, but deep son, dig it as deep as you can."

*   *   *   *   *

The Priest forgot to sleep, to eat or even to care about his appearance. Each week the standing room in his church increased for each of his remaining parishioners. There was no longer the need to use one's elbows to find the right spot on the floor. He had given up speaking from the chancel where he had been hidden from sight, preferring to stand with his people where his sermons took on a more forgiving mood far removed from the fires of Hell and damnation. God knew there was enough of the Devil's work abroad in daylight let alone when he stalked the lanes at night. Parishioners passed by, heads down, muffled across their faces and afraid to stop and talk in case the foul miasma was drawn into their lungs. The main street became piled high with horse manure as the situation turned from dismay to total bleakness when Zeke the Blacksmith died, falling over his forge in his weakness. The smell of cooked flesh wafted through the Smithy causing his wife to collapse on the front steps.

Meanwhile Jed dug and did not stop digging. The carts arrived at night spilling the sacks onto the ground like so much wheat waiting to be sown. But this also was a harvest, a harvest of souls, many of them caught short in the expectancy of their lives, most expiring in extraordinary, unrelieved pain. Jed dug because there was nothing else he could do: besides there were so few able-bodied men left to complete the work.

Then came that Monday morning. The Priest had slept, exhausted, head on a pillow laid onto his table when the sun prized open his bleary lids. Something was dreadfully wrong. People were talking outside, and loudly, oblivious that he might have been woken. He stumbled, stiff-jointed to the door and flung it open in despair. "What now?" He demanded.

"Father! Father! No new cases for a week now," shouted a woman in a clean white linen barbet and a smile as wide as her face. The Priest wrapped a blanket around his scrawny shoulders and turned to the woman. "Heaven be. But it may be a false dawn. The devil has many ways of winning his battles."

"Good day Father Thomas," came a voice behind him. The noble Lord had joined the group. Jed touched his forelock.

"You'll be able to get back to cutting my ditches and corn instead of graves, Jed, from the news I hear. That will bring food to your family."

"I've no family left, my Lord. I'm all alone now."

"Er, quite so. Well, there's a lot of work to do on the Estate. You can-"

"Beggin' your pardon, Sire. I am not sure I want to continue work on the farm. At least, not on a penny a day."

"That's the King's decree, Jed, not mine."

"'As might be so, my Lord, but I will have to do the work of three men now, so I need thru' pence a day from now on."

"Ha! And who would pay that sort of money, my lad, even supposing I would break the law?"

"My question is, Sire, if I don't do the work then who will? I reckons we now sets the rate."

The Priest shifted uncomfortably in his sandals. The world had turned upside down that Monday morning. Life would never be the same.

*   *   *   *   *

Thomas could not believe he had been spared when over half the clergy in York had succumbed. And the Lord of the village had survived and was even now awaiting news of the end of the scourge so he could marry his love, Elizabeth de Elton. She, also, God is good, God be praised, had survived.

"I believe, my Lord that making Jed a freeman might go some way to alleviate this problem-"

"I'll not be blackmailed Father-"

"No -one is suggesting this, Sire, least of all Jed, but you can see his point, repeated hundreds, nay thousands of times in the country. Each healthy man will have to do the work of three."

His namesake, Thomas, knew in his heart the Priest was correct in what he was suggesting." Hmm, and less people to feed, more money in the purse, more to spend." This was England's strength, to return quicker and much stronger than before.

The Priest in his sermon likened it to the great biblical flood when the world was cleansed and renewed. He sighed deep inside himself. His very beliefs had been shaken to the core for he had seen the youngest, most innocent children die, yet God had saved the two ruffians who lived in a clearing in Fox's Wood. They had taken up camp there planning to search for anything of value on the corpses but Jed had seen that each grave was back-filled and tamped down hard. None had been disturbed.

"All this to-ing and fro-ing for these burials from T'orp Arch really is a waste of time. And for why; because of an ancient agreement which has no meaning today? We need our own font and our own burials. We need a composition from St. Mary's and the Holy Angels. We need them to allow us to carry out our own Rites. Before the Great Pestilence we had the obligation of carrying corpses all the way to T'orp." It was Thomas Fairfax, the keen, eager scion of the family, willing to build bridges after the turmoil earlier when the Plague had decimated the population and caused violent rifts in the relations between Lord and servants.

"I will make a journey to T'orp tomorrow and speak with Robert, the vicar. I will then make a journey arrangement to go to York to the Sacristan on the matter."

"Thank you, thank you Sire."

"No need to thank me Father. I've lost most of my family. I need clean air and a new purpose in life again."

"There is still the small matter of the Reverend Mother at Monkton."

"Yes, Monkton, God bless them. They will be the ones who will have to find funds for the vicar in T'orp." The two men nodded their heads in agreement. It was as if the terrible plague had focussed all their minds towards each other, each acknowledging in the other a new respect for their station in life. Each had moved slightly but firmly towards the other; life was changing for both of them, mutually recognising that they both needed each other in a way that hadn't existed before.

Chapter Four

Treason or Disloyalty

Little did either man know that within forty years, just as Thomas had predicted, Waleston would become a thriving, prosperous place to live, placing T'orp Arch in its shadow as it began to take the initiative. The Composition finally arrived allowing the village to take care of its own baptisms and burials and a stone font was cut. The font was neither the best design nor using the best skills available in the world, the Priest knew, and it didn't even have a drain hole for the Holy water to escape, but there would be time in the future to find something better. In the mean time it was essential that they had the tools to carry out the new permissions and a poor font was better than just the floor space it now occupied. It was lined up with the devil's door and the people proudly strutted the stone slab floor after the market, patting the stone faces in pride and satisfaction. The new arrangements did cost Monkton Priory three shillings and four pence, split in half and paid twice a year to Thorp's Priest but the issue had drifted away as these things always seemed to do over time, allowing the nuns to fall back into their regular way of life with the growing of peas and beans and tending their cows and goats. Waleston threw off renewed attacks of the plague as if those left from the ravages of the first epidemic had been marked specially by God as worthy of keeping upon this world. Jed became a freeman and began to earn more than thru'pence a day as the shortage of labour was felt in the Great

Hall. New barns began to take shape like skeletons emerging from their graves and new stone was added to the old, retained part of the tower to match it in with the new church. As the sun began to set on those summer evenings and nightingales came out to sing in the hedgerows, St. Peter's did indeed glow like Jerusalem. A visiting traveller, full of relics from the Holy Lands was amazed when he saw the sun upon the south wall of the church.

"It must be a sign," he declared as loudly as he could for the villagers in the north, hereabouts, were suspicious of strangers purporting to be from Tyre and Sidon and the Sea of Galilee. His sales had been, up until now, meagre to say the least and he needed a bite to eat.

"A splinter from the Cross; a piece of cloth from the tomb itself. I have here," he held up a muddy piece of wood, "a knuckle bone from St. Thomas à Becket his'self."

The incredulous crowd surged forward to look at his wonders as he drew them from a leather bag one by one, pausing between each one to allow the richer ones to calculate if they could afford such a holy relic, one which would ward off evils even at night.

"There cannot be much left of the Cross by now," one wisecrack shouted from the back. "You are the fifth this year saying yours is the true Cross."

The throng laughed. It was good entertainment: besides, what if this one *was* the real thing?

There came a flutter of movement behind them. William Stockdale, shoe maker pulled two of the elders out of the crowd and hustled them back to a fence.

"John Fairfax has died; died in his sleep, God rest his soul," they were told about their Rector in hushed tones. There was a flurry of hastily performed crossing of chests.

"He must have known he was going to die. What, it was only two months ago he said he wanted to put coloured glass in the nave windows."

"He had asked to be laid to rest beneath the floor of the church and that we accommodate further members of his family in the future in the same manner."

"*Reqiescat in pace.*" The second man pulled his cowl closer to his neck as if to ward off death's sickle. "There is only enough space for half a dozen bodies."

"Then we will honour his request until the ground below the chancel is full. But, we must take up the floor carefully for it is only fifty years old and in good condition."

"And, of course, we shall need a new Priest."

The thought troubled all three men. It was always a problem getting just the right man for the job; neither too worldly so that he rubbed too familiar shoulders with his flock in the inn nor too godly that he set himself on a plane where no-one understood him. Too much Latin only led to confusion and ignorance, though with the power of the Fairfax's behind them the decision might well be imposed upon the village.

William looked back up the green hill to the church. He had been told it had been a hard slog, with long faces at the time when it seemed as if the money would never be fully raised. Course after course of the creamy stone had been laid in a deep lime mortar bed so that the material would be able to move without cracking as it shrank in the summer and expanded in the winter frosts. Several times, the story had it, Jethro, the original builder of the church had ordered work to be taken down as it '...simply wasn't good enough.' He was right for, in several areas, the stone walls had risen out of plumb and it would not have been possible to build in the flat-headed windows if the builder had not put his foot down at the opportune moment.

Then had come the glorious day when the building was complete and it became a church and now his baby son would be baptised in Waleston rather than down the road at T'orp Arch.

He studied the noisy crowd still bantering with the traveller. Many were well shod by his own hands and he had picked up more trade from the nearby villages because of his skills. John, one of the elders with him had been a thatcher until a fall had prevented him from climbing any more ladders. Far fewer tofts now had leaks: the wealth flowed as if it were a river up the main track from York where, he had been told, the Cathedral would still take another hundred years to complete at the speed it was being built. There was some confusion in the minds of the uneducated serfs that York was described as a Minster but, to them it was the largest cathedral in the whole known world. What they did not know, nor even the builders of the enormous building, was that the central tower had begun to become unstable. Hardly a day had gone by when news came, via a fast horse, that the main tower had collapsed, leaving mountainous piles of broken stone and a column of lime dust rising into the sky like a giant mushroom. It left a hole to the sky where God, undoubtedly still looked through daring anyone with the temerity to consider rebuilding, to think again. Perhaps it had been too high, said some? Perhaps man was never meant to build to the heavens. The devil had certainly won another round profoundly upsetting the forces of good, and there was much shaking of tonsures as to what to do in the future.

The people of Waleston, isolated in the countryside from the politics of the great city, shivered at the warning that if ever they were to build a higher tower themselves they should always remember the lessons of York.

To William, the height of St. Peter's seemed just about right. Its four stone pinnacles could be seen for many a mile and there was no money anyway, even if there was the will, to plan something even higher. It wasn't as if such a structure could hold any more penitents, and it would merely be a boastful arrogance of how good and great the village had become.

If he had known of the stirrings in the land, the unrest and unhappiness, of land jealously guarded, of boundaries and border talk, of Kings and Claimants, he might well have held on to his purse even tighter.

The mood was changing once again as if it tried to match the seasons which governed all of life in the countryside. While minor scuffles and armed skirmishes broke out, both sides in the argument hardened their attitudes. Men in the village met to discuss their allegiances which swayed like a Whitby boat in the sea as the fish came up heavy in the net. How to choose and who to choose became the over-riding questions on every man's lips while the womenfolk shook their heads in dismay knowing the cruelty which was to follow in its wake. As if the Black Death had not wreaked sufficient destruction, now the future held only similar bleakness and loss.

While Henry V had reigned, his strength had held the country firm from the envious eyes of the Yorkists, and in particular, those of Richard, Duke of York.

The jealousy threatened to swamp the village as a picture began to emerge from the doubt and distrust. The people did have a king, crowned in London before witnesses, establishing the House of Lancaster: yet, on their doorstep sat Richard, with very similar claims to the throne.

*   *   *   *   *

For a time the issues rumbled on: then Richard quarrelled openly at Court. Horsemen were seen on the Wetherby road and later, returning to York; urgent men with lathered horses, faces cowled and grim as they sought to deliver the imperatives of claim and counterclaim. The road became even more pitted if that were possible, as the traffic increased. The only positive element arising was the disappearance of the footpads from the main roads. Too many of these messengers were well armed and well able to take care of themselves, ready to kill to ensure the letters were taken through to their lawful destination.

The women walked in twos and threes up to the well to discuss the hopelessness of the situation. "No-one will move, no-one will try and talk," said the shoe-maker's wife. "If we were to run the country this land would be richer and happier."

The men folk smiled, for their women were ignorant of the great politics seething like a bee hive in late summer. "If only they knew the real situation, then they would stop their cackling and perhaps we could get our meals when we wanted."

But to man and wife alike, the fear grew, that whoever they supported, it might be the wrong choice. You were either for the King or for Richard, leaving nothing between. It simply was not possible to say '...let them fight it out,' for this provoked cries of 'treason' or disloyalty to the men at the Manor down the road. Whichever way the logic flowed, death winked them in the face, causing Lucifer's hand to strengthen, happy as he was to be back in full vigour for the first time since the bad days when people's faces turned black and their skin split apart with the pus. To most, God was the only sane voice in a big wilderness.

"William...William Fairfax. We'll have to remain loyal to him. He's well...Waleston isn't he?" It was Roger the cissor, sitting on his usual bench outside his toft, stitching a leather apron together from small pieces he had saved. His gnarled fingers followed the progress of the needle having no time to regret the onset of arthritis. His tights were pulled up almost to his waist and his tunic was opened wide at the front.

"There you go again, against our lawful King," said his wife, a buxom lady well below his own age. She threaded a new piece of cord onto another needle.

"Perhaps, but many say he is not really our King, that his ancestors are no more pure than our own Richard."

"Well, who ever," she grumbled, "but William Fairfax is a Yorkist and he will ask you to wear a White Rose."

Roger pricked himself at the thought of being pushed into a corner he could not escape from. A thought came to him. He sucked his fore finger noisily but received no sympathy. "I'm too old to fight but I could attend the army. I could supply new leather jerkins, trousers, aprons and the like. And repairs: their own clothes take a lot of beating in a battle. We could be rich, Catherine and build on an extra room to the toft; rent it out. It is only a matter of time before a great battle will be fought in the north where all the trouble came from in the first place, so we would not have to travel far; on our threshold, so to speak."

Roger had no idea how prescient his words would be as the deadly truth began to unfold in front of the village. He got word of a fierce battle in the south at a place called St. Albans and the village cheered when they learned that Richard of York had defeated Somerset's Lancastrian army and killed him in the process.

But, the force for evil was still at work, as Roger, planning to rendezvous with the army at Wakefield, not a day's ride for him, received the news that a great battle had already been fought there and Richard and his son Edmund had been killed on that bitterly cold night one day before the end of the year.

Waleston immediately headed for depression as they realised how quickly the fortunes of war could be reversed and what seemed a triumph only a short while before, now appeared as if all was lost. The villagers were fearful for their own lives if the army showed any inclination to march any further north. Wakefield was but a day's forced march and soldiers could be in Wetherby and thus the surrounding villages, looting grain stores and stealing their animals in order that the men were fed. The idea of stitching tabards for a victorious army tasted sour in Roger's mouth and he set to with all the able-bodied men in the village to bury as much grain as possible. Cutting holes in the ground to hide the sacks was back-breaking work for winter had set in well and truly and the soil had frozen like iron in the blacksmith's forge. The older men sniffed the air smelling snow on the way, warmed only by the news that Richard's eldest son, Edward was on his way north with a new army.

*   *   *   *   *

It was almost at the end of March, when the snow began to drive across the hills, to force icy blasts through the door frames and cause smoke to blow down the chimneys. Water butts froze and those animals left to survive the winter steamed in the wattle and daub buildings that provided home for man and beast. The first they knew of the awful battle was when villagers from Towton, just six miles away began flooding along the road with their miserable possessions, driving a cow or a couple of goats in front of them. Some had a chair on their shoulders as if that was any use to feed the children trailing behind; others had a blanket and a shovel, or a pan and firewood.

Most did not want to stop and talk though a few, more brave than the others, took a cup of water gratefully. They spoke, quickly, however, of ridiculous numbers of men being killed, a consensus being of twenty-eight thousand, but that would have been a quarter of the combined armies and that just could not be possible. Some had died on what was immediately named Bloody Meadow. Many had panicked and run away only to find themselves trapped in the marsh running alongside a small river known as cock Beck. One spoke of Edward's clever plan to site his forces so the snow blinded the Lancastrians eyes even as the strong wind also favoured his archers, staying out of range while they waited to fire.

Edward was triumphant and Waleston's grain and animals were safe, as Henry fled north to Scotland.

* * * * *

In the next few days, more and more terribly injured men began to arrive in carts and on foot. The village could do little other than to give them water and soup and clean their wounds. John Esdike, the Priest, could not believe the ferocity of Englishman against Englishman. As he bathed feverish brows he listened to the stories of Henry's men, terrified in the blinding snow, unable to tell friend from foe and unable to recognise even their Nobles banners. Exhausted from fighting all day they had run to what they had thought was safety only to find themselves up to their knees in glutinous mud which sucked at their legs like greedy piglets to a sow, and eventually for most, disconnected their souls from their bodies. So many died of wounds to their backs; an arrow head in the spine, an axe wound in the nape of the neck. There was no sense of victory for even as it had been with Roger, it left a taste of shame on John's lips as he sent yet another soul fleeing to heaven.

Some continued to affirm that twenty-eight thousand had been killed or died of their wounds over three days, most on that first dreadful snowy morning. Whatever the figure, it reflected the horror of civil war, felt John, thankful at last that the survivors had moved on, the battle carts piled with awful pieces departed and the cries of the injured, calmed in death.

"Where," he called out in his sermon the following Sunday, "where has it all gone so wrong? We are taught to turn the other cheek, to love thy neighbour, yet the bodies pile up so high, frozen to the ground that it is impossible to bury them."

His congregation stared up at him wishing they could have sat down while they received his stronger than usual mauling, but he wasn't going to let them off lightly and it took another hour before they were permitted to move from the graveyard cold of the church to the biting wind on the slope down to their homes.

Adam Swynhird summed it all up in the Black Bull. "Henry is still alive, they say, and safe in Scotland. If he can build another army he can come south again, and Waleston is right in its path." His chilling words turned the cider to vinegar. "When is this all going to end? Towton should have settled this forever, certainly with the number of dead lying out on that field. This argument on just who is our rightful king has already lasted six years, how much longer?"

No-one of course, could answer him. Their wives were sick of the death and the smell of fear which even managed to override the usual body odours created by heavy clothes in winter time and the general lack of washing. But life continued to surprise the Priest. While the war waxed and waned across the whole country, each sided locked in a monumental struggle for possession of the throne, a miracle happened.

*   *   *   *   *

John was tending the herbs in his garden, weeding the goose grass which had coiled around his pea sticks, when he received news from St. Mary and the Holy Angels in York inviting him to the consecration of the new Minster. Spring warmth was beginning to soften the ground as he set off on his horse with his boots polished and his cloak well brushed.

"Two hundred and fifty years to build Father," said an invited stone mason proudly, detailed to look after the Priest. The artisan's head was covered in a black velvet cap which fitted his skull tightly tending to pull his eyes into slits. That suited a man who worked with flying chips of stone throughout every daylight hour. "The towers are sixty two yards high, the highest in the whole of God's world. Do you know Father it is one hundred and seventy five yards long?"

Father John made the mental comparison, as he must, with this earnest man beside him, with Walton's seventeen yards in length. Over ten times longer in York His mind could not get around the fact, yet here it came into view as he crossed the bridge, walking his horse.

It was as if man had, indeed, decided to build right up to God's threshold. John became fearful for the man or men who had dared to challenge the heavens. This had never been attempted before and no-one knew just what they might find when they climbed to the top. The exquisite tracery glowed in the creamy stone showing a skill that his own church's masons would never be able to match.

He walked inside throwing off his cloak and its weight on his shoulders. Immediately, the street chatter died to nothing as if a giant cloth had been wrapped around the creation. The sheer volume of the interior drove the air from his chest and the presence of something very powerful made him cast his eyes to the floor in fear of looking directly into God's eyes. Monks and clerics moved without a sound as they strode constantly in and out of the beams of coloured light. At one moment they could be seen as if they were Joseph in his coat of many colours, the next, black on black, they were gone, vanished into thin air as if being snuffed out like a candle. Then, one or more would reappear as another window was crossed and the process repeated itself. It was almost magical thought Father John but he reprimanded himself fiercely as he recalled the fact that God himself had created this building as He had guided his stone masons ever upward towards the roof and towards His own house. This was not magic, merely that the effect produced a magical aura.

It came to him, as he celebrated Mass later in the day that just one hundred and seventy miles away, fighting and killing, pain and anger with so much loss of blood were being vented as two kings and eleven thousand men still slogged it out for supremacy: this time the chosen field was at Tewkesbury. When the Priest learned, a month later of the savagery laid by the Yorkists against brother Englishmen, he shuddered at the utter depravity sweeping the land.

*   *   *   *   *

John Esdike, Roman Catholic priest of Walton, lived to see the end of the war although it would be another fourteen years before it all came to a halt in the simplest way. Both armies were English; both used the same weaponry and could cross the country with familiarity as easily as the opposing force. It was likely the war could last for generations, the only change being the gradual increase in the ferocity of the exchanges. So Henry

VII decided to change his tactics with an offer of marriage to Elizabeth of York. Miraculously the fighting stopped and in so doing a new dynasty was created.

In Walton, the habit of shaking a head as a sign of confusion was to be seen everywhere. Men had fought men for twenty-nine years, on and off. Previously, events had been settled by a show of superior force; from today it was by a tryst in a bed. Henry Tudor, a careful man with an eye to the purse strings was here to stay. And, while all this was happening in London, the far-away capital, Thomas Fairfax became a Knight, with his shield displaying Walton and Gilling as his homes.

*   *   *   *   *

Peace, despite the uncertainty did come to the village. John, ageing now, but with the memories of his first visit to York undiminished, had been determined that law and order should return to the countryside. Since his journey to the great Cathedral, the roads had been reduced to impassibility except in high summer. Neither did anyone dare to travel except in groups and in broad daylight. No-one was that stupid to travel from Wetherby to York on their own, for while they might arrive it would not be with their purse. The King wanted law and order to return, so did the village, and its Priest saw fit to ensure his parishioners obeyed the Ten Commandments.

In a series of sermons he began to reign down fire and brimstone as he lashed out on everyone whether he believed they had transgressed or not. Mary, a spinster who wove fine cloth for well-born clients was at first upset on being included with the motley especially the young yobbos who sat on the church wall with their feet dangling down in a most unruly fashion and ate apples of a suspect origin. But, as time went by, the main road revealed less and less incidents of robbery and theft of cattle or the killing of the Lord's deer. There was to be no tolerance with those who transgressed the wish of the village.

The punishments, though, John realised far outweighed even the most heinous of crimes of theft, yet those that made up their minds to continue breaking the law risked the most dreadful retribution. Who would risk being found out and caught when the only result was to be hanged for stealing a single sheep?

When the wind lay in the south-west, which it most-times did, it passed through and around the rotting cadavers creaking as they caught the wind currents giving the crows time to make their pick of the choice pieces on offer. The stench of rotten meat from the gibbet on the Wetherby Road gave rise to dark jokes about how long it would take a hanged man to drop to the ground as the noose wore out. And when the wind really blew, the residents could gauge its strength by the clatter of bones stripped clean of any flesh. If the wind had changed course it often made no difference for the town had another gibbet on the other side of town to remind arrivals from the north of what lay in store for those who transgressed the law.

After John Esdike departed the human race having seen at least one wonder of the world, he was succeeded by William Ranald a clever, sharp man filled with the saintliness of God but who was unable to ward off the ravages of consumption. He died before he had had time for his cuffs to polish the top of the lectern; and never had the time to learn the names of his parishioners.

Upset at two deaths in such a short period of time, Walton chose Miles Stockdale. The new Priest made a first call at the Great Hall where he made an impact on his Lordship by demonstrating his knowledge of guns for game and then, later, by his accuracy in firing them, bringing birds down with considerable ease, much to the pleasure of the younger boys in the village.

He would often be seen in the village sitting on a log with his hands folded over his ample stomach, for therein lay his greatest weakness: food, and plenty of it. Father Stockdale loved food. He had had his fishpond widened and deepened, the latter to keep the herons away, so it would take many more pike and carp; his barn too was also extended so it could contain a dozen more chickens and their resulting summer egg production. He had two pigs which, every time he visited them would bring his lips salivating reminding him of the tasty meat and crackling with bacon chops and a gammon to carve in addition. His housekeeper was asked constantly what new dishes she could conjure up, which at times threw her to distraction. She felt obliged to make the rounds of the village asking questions on how best to cook a goose or broil a fish to bring it greater flavour.

Life was indeed one long round of dinners and suppers and, in between, a pie or a chicken leg or two to keep the growling from his stomach. Invitations for him to come to lunch would be delayed solely because of the need to give his sermon on Sunday and the occasional burial or baptism to break the routine of the year.

He had been blessing the harvest for five autumns when news arrived of the death of Henry and the coronation of his son, also named Henry.

"Henry the..." he ran his fingers across both hands. "Henry the Eighth, it must be," he calculated correctly. "I wonder what such a young king is going to bring us?"

Privately, the Priest hoped that whatever plans he might dream up in his palace it would not be put into action anywhere near Wetherby or York. The country was settling down now, free of war, more law-abiding again with the wool trade flourishing. It did not warrant further change or taxes to be levied on the populations in the north, decimated as they had been for such a long time.

His thoughts ran loose as a sack of corn on a rat hole. The grand ideas, the freedoms hard won began to spill across the threshing floor as they learned that the eighteen year old King had rapidly found out how to hold and deploy his power.

Chapter Five

Dissolution

By the time Miles Stockdale died and his weighty body born by six strong farmers' sons was interred in the church yard overlooking the fields and beyond to Fox's Wood, Thomas Dikson had taken over the reins of the successful village.

On his arrival, like most of his predecessors, he went straight to the church and entered alone through the south door. The nave was silent save for the mewling of swallows swinging through the tie-beams of the wooden trusses. Thomas looked up at the paintings on the walls of the nave and the bare, swept paving of the floor. The sun at that moment chose to break out of the earlier, leaden sky to send a narrow beam of red and blue light through the two main windows. Turning his back on the ancient Norman door leading to the tower he studied the better than average wood carving of the rood screen which separated the nave from the chancel, and the parishioners from the service. Why, he had challenged his mind all of his life on the subject, had it been decreed that the people whom Jesus loved equally, been barred from joining in the service...the '...worship proper' as one old charcoal maker had put it? And, why was no-one permitted to sit, other than the clergy, when they were usually fit enough to stand but the aged ones in the village obliged to stand for an hour or more? Surely everyone should help each other? He had heard that a few churches in East Anglia, the bread basket of England often having enormous wealth had now installed seats. The savage cold and bitter winds needed to be held at bay by seats or benches with screens to their backs to make the hour long service more tolerable. They were to be called pews.

Looking around he could see there were three small altars in the nave each with a lamp trimmed and alight for his arrival. They were expecting him but with no idea what time he might turn up, if not tomorrow, they had gone back to work. He felt welcomed and gratified with their gesture.

On the other side of the screen with its well-carved crucifixion scenes, the chancel smelt of trapped incense and candle smoke. Coloured light poured down from the large east window. As it did it bounced off the white cloth and polished brass on the stone altar cleverly drawing in the eye as it did so. Thomas nodded to himself. 'This will do', he thought, for great changes were on their way in the land, blowing up from the south, soon to absorb the county and its people.

St. Peter's would be no different from any other church in the future where there came a pressing call for the people to be far more involved in the service. Clarity was the by-word and the monks and clergy found it daily more challenging as they attempted to answer the pressing and even downright rude questions now being raised as a matter of course.

'Why,' they would ask, 'was everything chanted in Latin, when this was England and not Rome?' The days had long gone when there was a blind acceptance of the edicts handed down from the Pope through his Priests.

He turned as he heard rapid footsteps to find two men, somewhat out of breath and red-faced, reasonably dressed though with long boots covered in cow manure. They stood still as he faced them, hats cradled in their hands.

"Morning, Father," said one. "We are your church wardens William Seton, 'tis 'ee, and me I'm Jeffrey Page. We 'eard you 'ad arrived and thought best we be 'ere to show you around. We 'eard you 'ad arrived earlier on your 'orse."

Thomas smiled to himself. Not an aitch in hearing. "It is not *my* horse Mr. Page. I borrowed it from St. Mary of the Holy Angels in York. It is my plan tomorrow to make an early start at the church and meet the village on Sunday. I plan to hold a small reception, some cider, some beer, apples for the children. Tell me, Mr. Seton, do you have many markets in the church these days?"

"No Father, none these days." The man folded his hat in his pudgy fingers each like a black pudding wondering why the question had been asked. "We have a large byre nowadays, not far away which does nicely for us on wet days so we do not have to wash the floor of St. Peter's as often."

Thomas smiled again. Their boots had not been washed either. "That is excellent news gentlemen. I want St. Peter's to lead in the future. One day I want to see this screen come down and the pulpit...pulled forward...here under the window so everyone can see me in the nave. And with the screen gone everyone will be able to see as well as hear our service. Here," he emphasized with a strong thrust of his arm into space, "where everyone can hear God's word."

If he had tried to shock his two church wardens more he could not have done so. William's jaw swung down seeking air as if he were emulating an ape. Jeffrey just looked at the floor discomfited for he had heard of these radical ideas coming up the Great North Road to York, but he felt it right to give a modicum of support to his new Priest. "The screen, Father, is only lightly fixed and can be removed with relative ease. Only some damage to the floor I believe. We had always thought of putting more fixings to the walls but there seemed no point as there is little traffic through the screen."

William tried to catch his colleague's eyes without the new Priest seeing him but was unlucky. It appeared as if Jeffrey was going along with the new proposals without even thinking about them. Of course, William thought to himself, it *would* be quite nice to have the service in full view of the villagers. He knew quite a lot of the men on a Saturday night in the Black Bull had made comment in the past on such an idea.

Surprisingly also, the King had not moved to dampen the enthusiasm of the younger clergy and there was even talk at Court that Henry was actively planning radical changes.

"But, this is a nice village, somewhere to grow and expand your ideas and to share them with the good people of Walton, but not too quickly on anything-" Jeffrey was cut off by a raised hand.

"Don't worry Mr. Seton or Mr. Page. I have no intention of doing anything unless I have the full approval of the good people of Walton. Without their blessing nothing will change at all unless I am commanded so to do by the King."

This was very good news to the two men. While the Priest was the second most important man in the village it was nice, nonetheless when they were asked for their advice on matters relating to their church. Both men, however, could hardly have failed to notice there had been no mention of His Holiness the Pope and his position in all of this, above and beyond the King, as Supreme Pontiff. But, as they showed the new incumbent around the village and introduced him to the people who would play a large part in his life they felt an excitement missing from their last two Priests. Here was a man who wasn't afraid to think for himself, whose intelligence did not permit him to remain subservient on any matter of dogma or entrenched doctrine.

They hurried on. "And your pond is well-stocked Father. There's geese and ducks aplenty, a good apple store, a large herb garden and your barn is five yards long. There is a bench to sit in the sunshine while you think on your new sermon."

"Aha, William, if I may call you that, Mr. Seton. My sermons usually come straight from the heart but I will take that seat in the sun willingly."

All at once he felt this *was* a nice village, somewhere to develop his ideas. "Let's be having a look at this fish pond William. I'm especially fond of pike cutlets or a nice carp. And while we are discussing my comforts, I will need a girl to wash my linen."

"Mary has already been told, Father. She will keep your house clean, pick up the walnuts and apples that have fallen, feed the pigs and search for the eggs. She's a good girl, if a little simple. And she's good with bees an' all."

"Those are the most blessed of all by God, William. Those with a sense missing of thoughts that do not wish to join themselves neatly together as, perhaps, a woman sews a bed cover together."

The tour ended at the Great Hall where the sound of shooting echoed through a small copse.

"Does His Lordship get much involved in our church?" Thomas enquired out of politeness as much as from a pecuniary interest. Such a man would make or break his living. He had been told earlier that Monkton tithes which included the Walton rectorial tithes were now to be claimed by the Crown and thus, Henry King of all England, himself, leaving less for the village. His superior had merely shrugged his shoulders when questioned, an expression of helplessness and of hidden worries yet to be transferred down the hierarchy of the clergy. All he had said was: "Momentous times, Father Thomas. You had best watch your back and manage your accounts with great care. Leave not a penny to be questioned and you will be safe."

A strange comment perhaps, but Thomas understood exactly the politics higher up the chain and he needed to keep his nose clean at all times.

*   *   *   *   *

Momentous was a word all too often used to describe anything out of the ordinary and Thomas had often found the word easily debased. It was, however, the exact word he sought when, several years later a series of events coincided, two of them frightening beyond belief, the other, a demonstration of the way in which God balanced the efforts of the devil for attempting to create such a barren landscape of fear and death. It was as if he had received the two hammer blows of the Easter Cross, one after the other as real as if he had had to endure the nails in his wrists and feet.

*   *   *   *   *

"But Rievaulx? It's a magnificent monastery, rich that is, in its administration of the lands. This is..." Thomas stopped for breath. The messenger's horse was lathered, its legs trembling with the recent effort and he led it to the trough while he read the long letter. Words tripped out of his mouth without realisation. "Monks gone...disbanded...monastery destroyed...lead and glass stripped." He turned to the cleric. "They had a cast-iron furnace there, probably the best smelters in the country. If that has been destroyed where will we get our plough shares from? They never broke, they were so strong."

It wasn't a very caring comment upon the demise of one of God's most marvellous buildings in England and one of the great wonders of the age. But, there had been only an Abbott and twenty-three monks remaining when the order had been signed. Thomas knew that despite the shocking loss of destruction, change was not only in the air but had been kindled into the bright flame of mad revolution, one which could not be stopped. It had already disheartened the village with its oft-distressing news; and more was to come. He was powerless to stop it even if he had wanted to, but there was no point anyway for it matched his own ideas to perfection just as when he had first put his views to his two church wardens.

Along with the letter was a carefully copied advisory document suggesting ways and means of calming the worshippers while making changes, small at first; then, if the people showed an interest in accepting the new liturgy, more could be done. Thomas wanted to remove the rood screen. By so doing his people would be involved totally in the church service and nothing would be secret or hidden anymore. He wanted seats for his congregation, for the aged and infirm, for pregnant mothers. He wanted to let the blessed light pour into the church. In one shift, by removing the screen, which had been there since the church had been built, that had hid the yawning, flatulent Priest and his acolytes from the enquiring eyes of the ignorant and the motley, illiterate worshippers it freed the people and make them equal...or at least, more equal than they had been, and, he felt, that was the message.

Thomas had been joined by a few of the villagers who, while maintaining the respect his position demanded, nonetheless had learned of the rumours of Rievaulx's downfall and needed to know more. Thomas was quick to confirm the truth. This was not a time to stand behind his cloth and announce some platitude or other.

"Then," said one, "Fountains will be next... then York itself. There's no end of these buildings in this part of the country."

The idea of pulling York to the ground after it had taken two hundred and fifty years to put it up was too preposterous an idea to contemplate. But then, so had Rievaulx. There was a mood about the King such that no-one dared to raise his head above the parapet, and it was still fresh in their heads that a queen had already lost hers as a result of his warped thinking.

*   *   *   *   *

While they muttered and pondered on the changes which would have bewildered a cultured man of letters, let alone an uneducated farm hand sitting eating his lunch, they could see three travellers heading their way up the hill. As they came closer they could see it was a man and his wife with a child that whimpered and stumbled as he was harried along.

"Might we ask you for some water?" Asked the woman who was wrapped in a blanket and a cowl drawn over most of her face. She was not from any of the neighbouring villages of this he was certain.

There was an inflection in her voice, some note that did not ring true. Thomas stopped the child and lifted the side of the hood which threw a deep shadow across its face. Tears had streaked his face leaving white runnels down the grime. It was a boy.

He dropped the cloth quickly. "You may have water but you must all come with me...now please. You cannot bring the plague into this village."

At his words all thought of the Dissolution was wiped from the men's thoughts.

"Plague! For God's sake they cannot come here." The man who had spoken raised a pole as if to ward off the exhausted family who began to retreat down the hill again.

"Wait!" cried out Thomas. "I will bring you water." And he walked back to his house where he found an old pitcher which he could afford to lose and a large chunk of bread and some cheese.

"God bless you Sir," said the wife. Her husband was too tired, too racked with pain to do anything but nod his thanks.

The village had turned out in force once the awful word had spread like brushwood cast on a fire. Thomas knew he could do nothing else for them even if he realised he had found his sermon for the following Sunday. Walton simply could not take another plague. Children were healthy and mothers would not allow even Christianity to come between it and their child. He risked alienating the entire community to the extent where they might have him removed from the pulpit if he was to press his point.

He looked up the grassy green hill to where his church sat, seeing the lichen on the stone. He felt part of the building, worn, weathered and battered but still standing, to give direction to these people who had elected to follow the teachings of Christ.

He started back to where his parishioners were standing, staring at him, a mixture of admiration for his foolhardiness and anger at how little their Priest cared for his own.

"If you have brought the plague, the Black Death amongst us again, Father, God forgive you, for we won't."

"You have placed our children in mortal risk," said an old woman, bent, wizened and able to recall the last time the scourge arrived when she was a young girl. Her eyes showed her sadness.

Thomas dusted his hands on his cassock and walked on, understanding dawning. For all his Ministry, all he exhorted through the church, taught to the children and explained to the elders, all that but, in the end no-one was going to stand in the shoes of the Samaritan. York might lay down the governance of their lives but it was as nothing if the village was placed at risk.

But as he passed by the crowd, his chin held as high as he could muster, his absolute belief in what he had done was the right thing, shone through. His people began to hang their heads in shame, one by one. No-one wanted to make eye contact with this man, for he was a person they could never hope to aspire to, to match his decency and honesty.

Chapter Six

Rearrangements

It was a few weeks later that Thomas attended a regular meeting at Monkton to discuss matters affecting the whole diocese. At such meetings, Thomas felt the weight of the church at its heaviest on his shoulders and most imposed upon. The plague had been yet another scare and it had moved on with the travellers. They had made it to Wetherby before the child first, and then his father had succumbed. Thomas had woken each morning to feel his armpits for soreness but none had come. He had lit his own candle, in thanks and knew it could only have been divine intervention which had prevented a transfer of the disease to himself. God had other plans for him, he realised.

"Father! Father!" The voice of his superior roused him from his reverie. "We have exciting news."

"And what is that Archdeacon?"

"We have, as you know, been reviewing carefully on the future of the spiritual and temporal needs of the villages. Walton has moved into a dominant position of late and has become a centre for good citizenship. This is, in great part down to your hard work. On the other hand, Thorp Arch has somewhat lost the way. They have become more worldly, more lordly and uncaring. I see that your Rectory is valued at £4–13–4d. Hmmm..." He drummed his fingers on the table waiting for the assembled men and woman to take notice of what he felt would be an important comment.

"There is a recommendation that the Parishes of Wighill, Walton and Thorp Arch be put down and that they be incorporated into either Tadcaster or Bolton Percy-"

"But, surely," Thomas began, but was restrained by a friendly wave of the other's hand.

"One moment, Father, please. Your enthusiasm does you credit but wait until I give you the whole story. The rearrangements would mean that Thorp Arch would be demolished."

There was a hush. The destruction of any church, raised with God's hand and guidance was always an event to still the loudest and most shrill complainants. "And this will require the revaluation of Walton Rectory...upwards." The Archdeacon rather liked the pause and effect and felt it could be used in the future in his sermons.

Thomas sat still listening to the protestations of the two representatives from Thorp Arch. They had not bothered to send a full deputation believing the meetings a waste of time. Now, those that had come were quite out of their depth not being at a level where they could take any meaningful decisions.

Thomas sat still, his mind engaged in a mental tug-of-war. On the one hand leaving the brotherhood of Thorp Arch, so close to Walton in distance and linkage through the lands and farming, albeit containing the many tensions which had arisen over the years, would be a hard break. On the balancing side of the scales it might mean greater freedom and higher tithes: but, to knock Thorp Arch to the ground, the shame of the townspeople after all that had been said of their superiority over their neighbour. But again, who knew how Tadcaster or Bolton Percy would treat their new enlarged family, equally forced upon them without much discussion. Would they want another mouth to feed in hard times?

The man was continuing. "Of course, the Commissioners may change their minds and, if so, it will probably take another hundred years before the matter is considered again."

So, it was still all up in the air and, whichever way the coin fell to the ground he really had no say in the outcome. Thomas smiled to himself and felt again, events rushing by and all he wanted to do was to climb back on his horse and be enfolded in the calm of the village.

"I will await further instructions, Archdeacon –"

"Yes, yes," the Archdeacon replied somewhat testily at the mute reaction. The man seemed not to care about what could be an uplift in his living and showed all of the fidget of a horse wanting to get on down the road.

"Very well Father Thomas. I will write to you with my instructions. And, remember, we want an especially good turnout for the Michaelmas Fête this year." The man patted his purse to signify it was far from full. Thomas ignored the gesture totally, refusing to look towards the man, suddenly sick of the richness of life in York with its dozens of clerics and scores of lay brothers buzzing around the central hive. Something had become lost over the centuries, gone missing like a valuable locket or an heirloom and even with the enormous changes now on-going it appeared as if it was merely a transfer of power from one group to another.

That night, Thomas dreamed. He dreamed of the tide rolling in, then out again reminding him of the immense amount of time which had passed by before His Saviour had walked on earth. Behind this sea were the rocks and beyond them was a cliff, a huge slab of stone. At its top, his hands on his ample hips was the King, smiling grimly as he saw his plan unfolding. Thomas tossed in his sleep as his mind sought a way of protecting his church to maintain his way of life.

*   *   *   *   *

By the time Henry had worked his way through six wives and a complete break with Rome, Thomas was an old man having outlived most of his congregation. He briefly saw Edward Sixth attempt to master the throne but this was a sickly man never destined for great triumphs and led, after his death to Jane's fourteen days in power before her head joined a mounting pile. 'Bloody Mary' lasted for five years before she died after a five year attempt to stamp her mark on this impossible to rule, country.

Thomas was succeeded by another Thomas who gladly welcomed the news that his country now had a Queen with a stout heart and a determination to sort the nation out once and for all. No-one, least of all the Spanish was going to dictate to her and strangely perhaps, the words were to ring true.

At the well in the main street, amazed at the constant flow of information arriving from London, villagers discussed the events rolling in as fast as quicksilver through a man's hands. It was so far removed from their own life that it was as if those who lived in the south were on another planet, or at least, the moon.

Thomas Brown picked up his well-polished stick the following day, now worn through daily usage. His arthritis had come to him early in life and progressed in fits and starts. As his right hand clasped the crook it showed the swollen knuckles on each joint making it ever more difficult to take hold of the ewer of wine on the Sunday morning. He turned up the familiar path towards the south door fumbling for the right key. Walking in, he was still struck by the pure light and the sheer volume of St. Peter's. Gone was the wonderful colour streaming in through the windows. Gone was the rood screen. The builder had been right: it had been a light structure, light enough for it to be removed with little damage to the floor and none to the stone work. It had ended up in the Great Hall. The walls glowed with the purity of whitewash of lime. It had been a bit extravagant, he had been told, but worst was the need to have all of the plaster hacked off the walls destroying the beautiful stories of the Bible. But it was a symbolic washing as it had been with Christ's feet and it made sure that not a single element of the Old Catholic way of life remained to remind them of what could have been if England had had a different King.

At that time it had split the village fairly evenly down the middle with the die-hard Catholics, recusants as they were now called, devastated by the changes, seemingly made permanent. There would be no going back. The loss of the mysticism, the incense trailing smoke in wild arcs through the church, the sheer...openness of it all with the vicar, speaking to his congregation from a raised pulpit in the nave were things that would take the simple farmers a long while to assimilate into their way of life.

Now it was John Page's turn, and he like most others in his community sensed the strength of the new Queen as she set about restoring the moderate Anglicanism of her father. It was clear, quite unambiguous and gave to him strength to argue his beliefs with the wilting number of die-hards supporting the Catholic faith. Even most of these gave up the uneven struggle when Elizabeth signed the Act of Supremacy to become the supreme governor of the church. Meanwhile, the Pope remained remote and threatening in Rome in all respects while England gave up its possessions in France, the port of Calais. It seemed to the English, like quite a good agreement.

John read the broadsheet sent on by a favoured uncle from London so he was able not only to keep right up to date with the latest political news but to pass it on to his Parishioners who drew upon the news greedily as a piglet sucks on a teat and marvelled at the speed of modern communications. He saw no point in England holding on to a single town in all the vastness that was France. It was, quite clearly one of their belongings and should have been returned long ago. Another headline declared he had a new Archbishop; Mathew Parker who was making sure his church was set fair for the future and his clergy fully in the mood of modern Protestant life.

The loss of the Pope's influence meant some members of Walton village would be obliged to attend newly designed services. If they chose, as some did to begin with, to stay away they were liable to a fine of one shilling for each week they did not attend. They were known to John and, as he stared down at the seated faces in the new pews he tried to read their minds. Their eyes were glazed, but then weren't they always. Some, a few, were closed, an attempt to shut out the fearful message: this vicar was uttering the words of the anti-Christ. A few, a very few, paid up until they moved. It was better, they considered, to be in France or Spain with all their own troubles than remain in this God forsaken country and risk eternal damnation.

Walton continued to argue and debate the rights and wrongs of these devastating changes until, at last, Robert Huddlestone arrived to fill the shoes of the vicar, a curate granted a curacy for life.

His predecessor had only lasted a year having never had the time to enjoy the comforts of a lifetime living, after the plague carried him off as quickly as a horse ploughs an acre of ground. One moment he had been there in his village, his characteristic, booming voice heard well across the street the next sunrise, the next, black pustules had made an appearance under his aching armpits to burst into suppurating sores. John Page the vicar did not live to see either as he succumbed to the terrible disease which came and went in the land as will-o-the-wisp on the marshes.

When Robert had first established himself he had feared that Mary might return to install her particular brand of Catholicism on the people, bringing with her a far more vicious back-lash this time as she sought revenge for Henry's triumphs over the Pope. It would be a disaster for England if, having made the monumental changes to the church they were to be swept aside again in order that this woman could satisfy her own personal caprice. There would be a settling of old scores and what, he wondered, would happen to the churches which had all gone through such upheavals? Would she try and reinstall the great monasteries again? Was there anyone out there who could build such monuments; create the coloured glass or the carvings in the rood-screens?

It was with God's grace that Elizabeth had been crowned before too much damage was done and the country moved into a new, more powerful period of its existence.

Robert Huddlestone was the type of Vicar that everyone wanted to have in his village. Like the shopkeeper or the publican they needed to fit into a particular mortise, just as a good picture is set within its border. They needed to have an ability to see everyone's point of view and to sway with the wind when it was found necessary as the elements stirred within them all. Robert was also a man set apart from his predecessors for an entirely new point of view.

Robert was to be a married man.

When he had accepted Walton as his new home he had made it clear he wanted to follow the new teachings first proposed under Edward Sixth. That Priests should marry. To the villagers, now inured to change, and having seen that change did not send them all to damnation and hell the idea was, they all had agreed in the pub, novel but no-one could see a reason why such a man should not have a wife to look after him. After all, Priests for centuries had had a house-keeper as part of the perks, and if the Priest and the house-keeper got up to non-spiritual activities from time to time, it was probably none of their business. Besides, they said, if the Archbishop of Canterbury, Thomas Cranmer could marry, and marry twice, then surely any Vicar could do the same?

Within two years Robert had found a woman, a young girl of twenty-three years with a strong back and a charm who would always engage with the village and help soothe many an argument. It was as if she was ideal for the post and Robert made up his mind before many seasons had slipped by, to tie a knot and marry Maid Matilda. Robert and Matty, as she was affectionately named were absorbed into the bloodstream of the village as easily as if they had grown a field of peas, removing the initial fears of the Vicar. In that summer they began to work themselves into the fabric of the village to remove any last shred of antagonism towards the idea of a Priest marrying.

It was well towards the end of October that an animated traveller driving an apothecary cart arrived in the main street where he set up his wares and began to shout out that there had been a mighty battle at sea. He was hoping for good sales on the back of his news. It was all about a huge flotilla of men-o-war, Spanish ships, the Armada as it became known, and Robert found, on quizzing the man that many of the Spanish ships had been lost after the main battle due to fierce storms which even down in Yorkshire had caused trees to bend from their main trunks. Such was the interest in Sir Francis and his clever seamanship that few sought to buy medicine and the salesman found fewer sales in return for his news. It was usually a good trade-off but today Drake was bigger news. God had intervened for the English removing the threat of a future invasion by destroying many of the Spanish fleet and its men. There was one story which spoke of the Spanish having more Priests on board their ships than seamen so there were insufficient trained sailors to fire the cannon, but the man of course, could not confirm the tale. What was clear was that Phillip's beard had been well and truly singed finishing off any remaining links that Queen Mary might have left behind. Catholics felt more than uneasy at the idea of England being invaded to reinstall their faith by force.

"I feel safer now," said Matty that night as she combed her hair for bed. Her long white night-dress was demure and chaste and reflected the pure whiteness of the material in the candlelight. "There was always that fear in the background, wasn't there, that the Spanish King, whatisname-?"

"Phillip dear."

"Yes, Phillip. Those Catholics have always been trouble and where would we be personally if they had invaded England? Your life might well have been at risk.,. being married, and all such.".

It was a good point, thought Robert, and as we have a woman as Queen, he should listen to his own wife more in future for the ladies always came up with the sensible ideas. "The English Navy is strong, stronger than anyone else, even the Dutch. You can sleep well tonight my dear."

And she did sleep and within two years bore him a son, later two daughters and another son. A small dynasty had begun in this small backwater of Yorkshire and was to continue for many years.

Chapter Seven

'But...I Don't Speak Latin'

It was almost exactly when the greatest Queen the country had ever had, finally died that the occasion was matched by another momentous event little noticed at the time but one that grew until it flowered eight years later. It arrived in the village through a courier from York, a sample of others to follow. There was an instruction with it to say that the Bishop's Bible was to be locked away and not used again without specific instruction.

The St. James's bible had arrived.

"This is astonishing," said Robert as he sat reading the black covered book with its English text. "This is simple amazing, Matty. Look, everyone who can read English can now read the bible."

"But, surely, that is the prerogative of the clergy...to control the flow of words from the Holy Book?"

"No, no, no my dear. The idea is to allow everyone, everyone in this village for example, to be able to follow the scriptures at home so it will not be just a case of hearing and learning from the Great Bible once a week. Now, anyone can take up the book at home and read it to others: something to do in all those long dark winter evenings." Matty, who found that she and Robert found plenty to do in the evenings when the children were asleep, smiled as she deferred to her husband's greater knowledge.

The next Sunday Robert walked down the nave aisle halfway through his service looking left and right as if for a face he recognised. He had, however, selected the person he needed to talk to before he had arrived. He espied the woman, the wife of a farmer who had spent long evenings teaching herself to read. He knew how much she had achieved for he had had her read to him on a number of times during quiet afternoons before the milking and egg collection.

"Elizabeth. Please come with me," he said quietly. She looked up quizzically wondering if she had heard him correctly.

"Please come," he repeated holding his hand out. Elizabeth rose and stepped around her husband William, bowing her head as she considered why she had been marked out in front of almost the entire village. She had done nothing wrong, of this she was sure but now she could feel seventy pairs of eyes on her head dress.

"Now", said Robert turning to the congregation, "Elizabeth is going to read from the bible, the Holy bible to you all. I have marked an extract for her."

"But...I don't speak Latin," she replied, dismayed at the vicar's request. But he was holding out a book, much smaller than the Bishop's Bible, and laid it on the lectern.

In front of the strangely mixed pair there was deep concern. Heads turned to each other, as eyebrows were drawn together. William stared towards the east window, aghast at the idea of his wife trying to read the bible in Latin.

Robert had opened the new book, a black leather cover with a simple gold cross on its front, to all intents and purposes a bible if a lot smaller than they were accustomed to seeing. The black print glared out at her. She could see it was the very first page of the Old Testament, Genesis.

"Now, Elizabeth, he said in a firm, commanding voice. "Read the first two verses. Hold your head up so everyone can hear you...it *is* important." He gave her a warm, encouraging smile of reassurance.

Elizabeth held her head up as instructed. "In the beginning, God created the heaven and the earth. And the earth was without form and void; and darkness was upon the face of the deep. And the spirit of God moved upon the face of the waters..."

There were audible gasps from her audience. Old Ma Hiley was so amazed that her toothless mouth opened to expose pink gums amid her simple face. "Lawks," she said to her neighbour. "The vicar has taught her Latin."

"No, no, that cannot be. How can it be? She was reading English."

Understanding dawned on the villagers even as Robert walked her back to her seat. Will rose to let her in somewhat fearful of the woman he had married seven years earlier, so much so he dropped his woollen cap on the floor. As he bent to retrieve it Robert climbed up into the pulpit.

"Now, dear friends. Can you imagine the miracle that has come upon us today? Elizabeth can read the bible, and the whole bible. She could have continued all day reading it to you until she reached the end of the Old Testament whereupon she could have started on the New Testament...that is before she had to stop to get Will's supper."

There was a nervous sort of chortle around the pews as the tension was lessened."As many as are here who can read, those will be able to read the bible in future." He stared down and round at the men's bared heads. Matty looked up, loving her husband even more at that moment. He held up the new book in his right hand opened at the same page. "And God said, let the earth bring forth grass, the herb yielding seed and the fruit tree yielding fruit after his kind whose seed is, in itself upon the earth: and it was so." He snapped the book shut with a bang.

"How those very words echo through this farming community of Walton. Soon, everyone who wishes will be able to read the bible at night, every night without having to speak to me to ask a question. Soon you will all become familiar with the good book and its written words."

Utter silence now. Not a sniff, or a cough, not a sidelong glance from a youth to a girl in the next row. It was as if his entire congregation was frozen in time as they sought to understand the disruption to their Sunday. Who, cleaning their boots an hour ago could have possibly imagined the future implications of this day, sprung upon them without a single earlier comment or warning?

When they filed out of the South door into unexpected sunshine with the previous rain shower still shining wetly on the stone slabs of the path they shook hands with Robert and said goodbye in subdued voices matching the time when the news of Queen Bess's death had reached them. In the road, free of the restraints' of the church boundary a gaggle of women surrounded Elizabeth and Will. They all attempted to speak first.

"How did you do it? Was it really English? You know, like we talk it? Was it some sort of trick, something you have learned by heart?"

At this last remark, the colour in Elizabeth's face, always ruddy from exposure all day in the fields, deepened. "No, Agnes It was just all there, so I could read it like a...a pamphlet."

The idea of equating a pamphlet or a poster with its doubtful truths with the Holy bible was unthinkable and Elizabeth realised she could have chosen a better comparison.

"Elizabeth merely means it is as clear as any book ever printed," said Will coming to her rescue.

"It was not in Latin," she interrupted with some force, "it was English as we speak it now."

Ma Hiley harrumphed loudly. " 'Tis not right, I thinks. We should not be able to read the Holy Bible, the holy words. That is only for the vicar."

"But why?" asked Elizabeth.

"Why? Why my dear? Well really, because...because... it is so."

"That is no reason at all is it Ma Hiley? As more and more people learn to read, more will be able to understand God's word."

"'Tis not right, methinks," the old woman repeated, grumbling, though clearly out of her depth faced as she was with the other women in the tight circle. The wooden frame under her dress trembled in excitement and she pulled at her coif as if it was tightening its hold around her head.

Henry Fairfax skirted the animated group swinging his stick wide as he headed back down the hill with his wife towards the Old Hall, deep in thought. He would have liked to have known about this King James Bible revelation before it was sprung upon them all in such a theatrical way, but he knew Robert was secure in the minds of the Walton villagers and, anyway, whether he liked it or not, the knowledge was now out in the open. Deep inside him he could see the future where people could read, could understand the scriptures far better and, if so, would understand the reasoning in a far more positive manner. *'The Age of Reason'*...he mused. It was coming, he was sure.

Like a performer's turn, Robert Huddlestone eventually stepped down to let his namesake Robert, replace his weary bones. This new man would find himself vicar of Walton for fifty years and live through the grimmest war in history.

Chapter Eight

Brother Against Brother

Robert Chambers eased his aching back which had begun to gnaw at his spine as if a stoat or a weasel was enjoying a nut. He studied the retreating form of his good friend Samuel. A frown moulded itself like drying clay on his forehead deepening and hardening as his bottom lip pushed upwards.

The two had had an argument, the first ever, for on most things in life they had enjoyed strong agreement. Samuel had helped support the church in every way he could and Robert had seen fit that his friend enjoyed his companionship. Samuel had never married, never even found a woman he might have considered to share the rest of his life with so his vicar brought conversation and engagement to a high pitch in his life. He had a neat and tidy mind, liking always to clear a point up before moving on; so much so he had grabbed a sickle one spring, a long time ago and over a period of four weeks, cut the grass in the churchyard. By the time he had finished, he had left the grass like the lawn at Hampton Court Palace.

The first area, the path side leading to the south door, had started rising up again like the tide. So, he had begun to cut it again and ever since cut the grass through the spring and summer months. It was a good relationship, one based on trust and neither pressed the other for anything more; until now, that is, when Samuel had departed noisily, stomping down the road between the cottages, muttering loudly to himself. "The King, God bless the King. We must support the King."

Robert turned away himself seeking solace in his church, seeing the future and fearing for his own people. The King, as he saw it, was clearly out of control having been corrupted, as so many before him, by the power foisted on him by an army of sycophants. He was taking on powers removing them from his people in a clear contravention of the rights of men. He was forcing through new Acts against the wishes of Parliament and had now summoned the Long Parliament as it was to become known. In a few short months the weak King had created constitutional, economic and political animosity, their combined sulphurous smoke blinding the rule of law and destroying the entire firm, unambiguous work of Elizabeth.

The ripples became waves all heading northwards where Charles rightly felt remarkably safe. York was Royalist through and through as they were in the west. It was only in London and the south that the Parliamentarians made their presence felt in no uncertain terms. Opposition grew like the wheat in the fertile valleys around York.

As Robert had first raised the subject of the King's lack of understanding of the wishes of his people, so Samuel, with better access to reliable information from the capital felt unable to agree with his vicar for the first time he could remember.

"I recall a time when another King, King John was brought to his knees by his nobles. He had tried to usurp their power: the Magna Carta defused the times and the mood," said Robert. "Surely the people of this great country should not be pushed aside like so much chaff in the wind, because of an accident of birth?"

"Accident! An accident? Without doubt you are wrong vicar. The King decrees and rules by birth, as part of the succession of power. His word, difficult as it may be to understand must be obeyed-"

"Even if it is wrong?"

"We are not party to His Majesty's plans. Soon he will reveal them to us, then you will understand."

Robert shook his head in utter frustration. "What you say, Samuel, if multiplied throughout the land will lead to civil war."

Samuel was not to be put off now he was in full flow. "So be it Vicar. The King's will must be done."

"Even if thousands die, brother against brother, father killing son?"

"Even so." Samuel had crossed a particular Rubicon of his own where there was, unfortunately for him, no place to retreat. "The King will never accept this Bill to curb the powers of the Bishops-"

"But it was passed in the House."

"By eleven votes only. That is hardly representative of the nation's wishes. That does not show our people supporting Parliament as it stands. I tell you Vicar, there will be many in this country, when they hear the news, who will now support the King in his just fight."

Robert knew of the Grand Remonstrance in the hunt for the limitation of power given over the years to the Bishops and the reforming of the church itself by employing the deliberations of a synod of Protestant churchmen. But, how did any of this matter in Walton, two hundred miles from the seat of that power?

"You simply cannot mean, Samuel, you would wish the death of your fellow English countrymen because one man speaks out in London?"

But Samuel had had enough and was unsure, anyway of the rocky path he had embarked upon. He was a roofer not a politician albeit he had always taken a deep interest in what was decided in the great city in the south. So he walked away from his friend unable to make up from the argument. That Sunday he was missing from his usual place in the church and his pew seat was left empty in case he turned up later. But, a week after the row, Robert noticed the length of the grass in the churchyard and knew he had lost a good friend.

As Charles raised his standard in Nottingham that August it was as if a stone wall came down in the road dividing the village into two opposing camps. There were two distinct parties in the Black Bull those days, the Royalists in the window and the Parliamentarians taking up the space to the rear, 'living in the shadows' as one wag put it. Conversation at the well head petered out as soon as one woman from the opposite side of the fence approached another group. Husbands began to argue fiercely with their wives despite Robert's exhortations to the contrary from the pulpit.

"Can you not see what this is doing to our community? What this is doing to us all? We are all taught to love one another and to turn the other cheek, but which of you can place your hand on your heart and say, '...yes, that is me Robert?' All I can see is a stubbornness and determination to be right, that all others are wrong and your will be done."

And after the service, he would be tackled on his sermon. "The Duke of Newcastle is raising an army in York, Vicar. A mighty force I am told."

"To fight and kill brother Englishmen is a sin, Jonathan," replied Robert, no longer willing to be subservient to his parishioners as he sought a way to reach into their anxious minds as the issue dominated all other conversation.

"It will be over and done with very quickly the man replied quickly. "The King has raised three armies, what with his own in Oxford and Hopton's in the south-west."

"I've never heard of a civil war that ends quickly Jonathan. Both sides have the same type of fighting man, both with the same weapons-"

"But the King has God on his side that is quite clear. The King has the just right."

Robert smiled gently seeing the queue begin to pile up behind the man and he shook hands and passed to the next concerned face.

Strange events at night began to occur. At first they were thought of as quirks, things that happen unexplained from time to time. Then it got worse. Pigs were mysteriously found in the orchards of their opponents. Chickens too disappeared without a squawk and with no sign of a fox. An ox was maimed, seemingly by a sharp end of a broken plough share. Further afield it became dangerous to open one's mouth or pass on by as if two dogs had circled each other as they sought a soft piece to bite but, failing to find an entry decided there were better things to do elsewhere.

Robert attempted to see all viewpoints and placate angry exchanges even as the country lurched towards civil war. The Scots, who in previous centuries had pillaged and raped across Yorkshire now sided with the Parliamentarians in exchange for land which brought an equalling of the forces standing to, pikes held aloft, like a palisade for a prized bull.

Night fell over the land and Walton shivered despite the summer heat.

In York, just twelve miles up the road the Parliamentarians began to besiege the town held by the King's men. As they did, half of Robert's flock were stunned to learn that Thomas Fairfax, a name they were all associated with through the powerful family which owned the village was leading the siege. Fairfax had led his men into Wetherby thereby stretching the resources of the small market town to the limits as his billeted men took what was available to them whether the locals were in favour of the situation or not. The carts, full of the weaponry of war, horse fodder and gunpowder choked the streets, with the resulting noise from the blacksmiths reaching all the way to the village. At night the sky glowed with their fires, lit all over the available ground where ever they found it convenient so to do, where they stood in groups their faces lit by the redness of the flames.

On the Second of July Prince Rupert, leading the King's men and his finest cavalry met with Fairfax on a wild meadow known as Marston Moor only five miles from Walton. A horse could reach it in under an hour, a well-trained army in two and a half. As the news grew, Robert's parishioners lost their bloody-mindedness as it became replaced with fear of death from either side indiscriminately. Why should a man be believed when he said he supported the King, to a group of nervous Royalist cavalry? Better to kill the man than receive a sword in the back later.

There was no doubt the ferocity of the Scots helped but it was a new Commander, fighting with consummate skill alongside Fairfax that won the day. The man's name was Cromwell and it would not be the last time that Robert would learn of that name.

As it had been one hundred and eighty years earlier, the village learned of the battle within the day. There had been confused news as the tide flowed on a bath of blood, no-one quite knowing which side held the day or even if the battle was over.

It had been evening in Walton, at about half past seven according to the His Lordship's time piece with the sky threatening a savage thunderstorm which then broke a few minutes later. It was the artillery which brought the villagers outside onto the road to the full awareness of a major battle taking place. John, a ditcher by trade, correctly interpreted the muffled thumps as being located on or near the moor.

"There are not many pieces being deployed, well, not yet anyway," he said doubtfully. "And it is difficult to say what are cannon and what is thunder."

"Aye" said another, "and we don't know whose cannon are firing either."

Two hours later, there came an eerie silence. The storm had cleared leaving soft washed daylight with late night birds resuming their perches after an unsettled evening. Eventually, a lone horseman stopped by briefly to tell Robert and a number of villagers that a great battle had been fought and won. "The enemy is routed," said the excited man still ahorse and preparing to ride on to Wetherby to find quarters for the night for his men and horses.

"Yes...but which side won?"

Surprised, the cavalry officer turned in his saddle. "The Allies of course. Rupert and Newcastle have fled, four thousand, methinks of their men are slain and we have captured all their ordnance, gunpowder and field kit."

But was this the end of it all, wondered Robert? Somehow he could not throw off the feeling there was yet a long weary road to follow before a conclusion, some sort of settlement was made to this awful war.

He had been on his knees in the church yard attempting to pick up the smaller stones and clods of earth following the mass burials. Royalist had been laid side by side with Parliamentarian: it didn't seem to matter anymore, for they all seemed so young and ready for life. Besides, they were all English. Now they lay crumpled and damaged in the stones of the moraine as cold as that ice which had brought it down from the far north.

A shadow fell across the long, straggly grass. Looking up he saw a mug of cider thrust out at him. Exhausted with it all he took it gratefully and shaded his eyes to see who it was.

"Thank you Samuel."

Samuel came and sat beside him not saying anything, just drawing on his own drink.

"Sorry we have made such a mess of the church yard. We are trying to clear it up but there were so many graves to dig and no-one really cared at the time. It was just necessary to get them into the ground," said Robert much comforted that his old friend was here beside him once again.

"That's alright vicar, I'll soon get this cleaned up. Then I'll cut the grass, eh?"

*   *   *   *   *

And while the war raged across the country the people of Yorkshire were split on two fronts at the same time. They had really no idea whose liturgy to support on a Sunday let alone the great issue of whether they were for King or Parliament.

Two weeks after the battle the village learned that York had surrendered, removing the Royalists main seat of power in the north. For those who had backed Fairfax this provided them with a breathing space and an ability to speak of their support more openly than they had in the past. It seemed so much more conclusive this time. The divisions in the ale house, the Black Bull, also collapsed as the need to have all hands to the harvest drew closer. War or no war, the people had to feed and if they missed the reaping they would all starve whoever they supported.

Robert survived the savagery and lived to see the restoration of the monarchy in the emergence of Charles Second. Did it really require a savage war for people to come to their senses, or rather, one man, the King, to see reason? It made no sense and there was a great wariness among the womenfolk of Walton who were frightened that having lost one King to a Republican another could follow.

"Keep your nose to the grindstone," said the Blacksmith's wife, Lizzie. As she gazed out through the forge door up the hill towards the Great Hall with a platter of bread and cheese for her husband, she knew it was just luck rather than God's grace that the village had been spared. It was almost as if God looked down occasionally to check progress then, if he espied peace or tranquillity he must need set these simple folk a new task.

"And you Lizzie don't get involved when you are out washing. Let sleeping dogs stay in the sun or below the table and don't step on them either."

"You should talk James, in that ale house of yours in the evenings. You men never seem to stop talking, do you?"

James wiped the sweat and iron filings from the ridge above his eyes as he accepted his lunch. Blackened fingers took hold of the fresh bread which crackled as he bit into the crust. A fine puff of flour settled on his upper lip causing Lizzie to run a finger across his face. "You keep working, doing your job and we will see out the troubles, just you mark my words."

The troubles did remove themselves one by one but a burning issue immediately arose with the new vicar, Samuel Wilson that is, in the opinion of most of the residents of the parish. The Reverend Wilson should never have been selected for the job but they had little say in the matter pre-arranged as it was by the Estate who owned the village. The man's face was 'sly' said one, like a 'weasel' said another, accentuated by the need for a razor to be applied, if only on a Sunday. His manner became more and more brusque as time went by as if he had tired of his job and wanted nothing better than to hunt and shoot...and to move on. Known to his Bishop for his attitude there was little chance of another posting for the unlucky man. His weasel words and ferret face barbed the congregation at a time when the vexed issue of what to do with Thorp Arch rose again to the top like foam on a river in spate.

Looking back, the Bishop could see it had indeed been a hundred years earlier that the question had come onto Thomas Dikson's table and nothing had been achieved. Now, here it was again and that 'evil' man as he had been described by more than one aggrieved parishioner might actually benefit from having success in the proposal. Reports were reaching him regularly of missed sermons, of missed services. Sunday school for the children had been abandoned and the latest account was that Wilson had preached only four times in the last year. Things had become intolerable he realised. With all this it would seem strange to say the least if the wretched man was to be rewarded with the annexation of Thorp Arch while making himself unpopular, unreachable and just plain rude most of the time. Slowly a plan formed itself in his mind, not one you might agree that God would have approved of but a necessity nonetheless... *'for the good of all...for the good of the community...'* all but one that was.

He began to work on the elements intent on reforming certain boundaries to ensure Wilson would not have his prayers answered. The Bishop was quite clear of what he was doing but would, he assured himself, seek absolution on the matter, but not until it had been signed and cleared from his desk.

Such a wrong choice of man for what, by necessity was a key role in the maintenance of the even tenor in the daily life of the village, thus removing worries from his own back yard, so to speak, meant that the vicar had to be removed, to disappear. Wilson fought like a weasel, grubbily, seeking recompense while refusing to carry out even the slightest of his pastoral duties. When he left, the whole village threw open their windows and doors as if to cleanse their houses from the unpleasantness the man had brought with him. There was a great washing of covers and Sunday clothes, the floor of the church was cleaned until the grains of sand in the clay floor tiles shone through as a speckle; brass gleamed and whistling was heard one day in the chancel.

Chapter Nine

A Crock of Butter

Mrs Westcott who 'did 'for the vicar and had put up with a very great deal of abuse by necessity, for it was a plum job and she needed the money, summed it all up nicely.

"New century...new vicar coming...new life," and welcomed Joshua Lancaster to the vicarage. His Archbishop, John Sharp noted his arrival and breathed a sigh of relief. He had spoken with Lord Fairfax who confirmed that, 'the £7-13-4 a year living was for a stipendiary curate. He has three and a half acres of glebe land laying in Thorp Arch and another half acre of tilled land also in that village. Then there is his toft and croft and a meadow which we value at three shillings.'

"That is quite as I see it," replied the Archbishop with a slight incline of his head.

"And, the dear man has a good home and a large barn. And he gets two shillings and sixpence for every marriage and eight shillings for a burial."

The Archbishop patted his stomach. It was tiring talking of such trivial matters though he had to admit that Lord Fairfax looked after his vicars in an ample way. Besides, the man's ancestors were all buried beneath the floor. Although there was no more space for future generations, the man had every right to run the place as he wished. One could hardly remonstrate with him on his choice of vicars.

"By the way, Archbishop, we have a shop, a real shop, selling everything, right within the village itself. The good man never sleeps I believe, such is the demand.

"That will be good for everyone. Less travel, less stocking up in the house."

"He also auctions property, organises the cricket and cock fights. He is the parish officer for funerals."

"Excellent. Money saved I'm sure and with pews for rent now at one shilling a year and what with window taxes at twelve pence a window everyone needs to save where they can."

"Perhaps, Archbishop, you might like to take luncheon with me. I am told there is a reasonable hare pie or perhaps some lungs in meat sauce, at the Unicorn-"

"Ah, the Unicorn. The food is good Sir and indeed, I would be pleased to join you, but perhaps, a seat at the back if possible. We should not show too much, er, flamboyance in these days."

The two rose, the Archbishop indicating his departure by patting his stomach yet again, this time for the benefit of his attendants.

*   *   *   *   *

Meanwhile, his ears burning, no doubt having been discussed, if from afar, Jacob Clough was discussing the future with Joshua Lancaster, his curate. The vicar had been anxious to know just how much work could be passed over to others without upsetting the village.

"If you can arrange funerals, are you able to supply gloves, hat bands, handkerchiefs...favours...and shrouds?"

"All and more vicar. You will not have to worry yourself on that score."

"But, we don't want too much betting going on, Jacob. It is against every tenet in the good book. As well as cockfighting, I hear they bet on cricket matches."

"Well, I do say you are right vicar. Cricket seems to draw out the spirit, the competition, I suppose. Almost everyone has a go. It is difficult to stop."

"As long as the betting is laid on Walton to win that could be more acceptable." The curate brushed his cassock seeing wind blowing down the road carrying with it a foul smelling aroma of human ordure from the cess pits. Pig dung, also lay in a great heap in the centre of the road where a lazy farmer had cleared up badly after his cart lost a wheel in a large rut. "And mind that strong beer you are bringing in. It brings such distress to some families."

"Yes vicar. I must get back for I can see Mrs Duall waiting for me."

"Goodbye Jacob and give my best to Mrs Duall."

Jacob hurried off retying his apron as he went. Outside the shop, in prime position, just fifty feet from the well, was a row of rakes, spades and rope coils alongside a string of rat traps hanging up from a beam propping up a lean-to roof which gave a shelter to shoppers. Ducking inside, due to his abnormal height he could see the woman concerned, studying a stand of brooms.

"'Ow much for one besom, Jacob? I ain't payin' a lot mind you."

"You have to pay what the price is, Mrs Duall. The price for one besom is, in fact, two pennies. I pay one penny to buy it and I sell it for two pennies."

Mrs. Duall sniffed as she studied the shop keeper below her substantial forehead. Her hair was scraped back into a tight bun. "Hmm. Too dear for me. I needs must go to Wetherby where I can buy them for a penny."

"As you wish Mrs Duall. Anything else I can do for you?"

"You ain't done nothing for me yet. I need a pint of them gooseberries and some sugar."

"Certainly." Mrs Duall had a lot more money salted away under her bed than she let on. Sugar was still a luxury and most in the village bought honey to sweeten fruit.

"And I'll take a broom, though I reckon you are robbing me at that price."

"Travel to Wetherby will cost you a penny, and then you have to come back. There's another penny. So you save a penny by coming to me."

The woman could not do the sums though there seemed a vague logic in the man's words. "That's thru'pence ha'penny please."

But she had turned and was fingering a box with a glass lid. "I can't see any papers in the box."

Jacob glanced in the tobacco box. "I'm making two hundred papers tonight, Mrs Duall. Do you want some for Mr. Duall?"

"'E does like 'em down at the ale house. 'E says they go together with the beer that is, like bread and cheese...and 'e seems to prefer ale to cheese these days."

"The tobacco will do him good, especially for his chest. It will aid his ailing cough."

"So they say," she replied as she counted out the exact money carefully.

As soon as she left, Jacob pulled a crock of butter, thirty nine pounds in weight from the cool store behind his counter. Setting it in a prominent position ready for cutting up he drew a blackboard to him and began to write carefully. He needed to rent out his second bedroom. A lodger for five pounds the year, he calculated, with full board naturally was good value, and it maximised the use of the house. He went outside and propped the board on an empty herring barrel waiting to be returned.

That vicar, he mused.. He needed to be kept out of the tight circle of men who bet on the cricket matches. After all, what was the point of a cricket match if you couldn't wager on the result?

The cricket was played on a cut section of the grass on the main meadow below the church yard. Joshua was able to gaze down on the game even as he wrote his next sermon. There was certainly a clash of wills over the betting issue and it had been decided to get the vicar to play for the home team on the basis it would be more difficult for him to object. The only problem remained, who was to ask him?

That evening, having rolled two hundred papers of Virginia tobacco, he took them round to the bar where smoke from pipes vied with the gusting fire. The men liked the fire right up to the end of June but as it grew hotter in the room the door was left open more often. The consequence was a series of draughts each night with the smoke from the logs refusing to draw up the chimney. When they returned to their respective beds their hair smelt as if they were smoked herrings. Jacob sold most of the papers and a pound of tobacco to the landlord before accepting a brandy. Life was full and good though he felt there was always more business to handle. He needed to find a woman, a wife willing to help out in the shop while he was away minding his other businesses.

The main talk that night was the confirmation that Walton was an official vicarage; not that it hadn't been before but there had been no clear cut document, no official declaration from the Archbishop that it was so. Joshua was determined otherwise and at long last his Archbishop had regularised the informal arrangement. He had placed a caveat, however, on his words for no-one could tell him what tithes were being paid on a regular basis, although one cleric had been able to ascertain synals of eight pence a year – and that was of no consequence to the church.

The regularisation was important to the people just as much as it was to their vicar for it set them above many other hamlets seeking to make a mark on the land, albeit small, a sense of pride in their efforts. After the war there was a time for reflection and a need to improve each and everyone's personal fortune. The official title bestowal added to that and allowed the men to stand a little taller as they bid in the market place. There was a mood too to clean up the self-interest which had abounded at the time of the Royalists. Joshua had seen the lowering in standards of the small, decent things in life and made it plain to Jacob in his shop.

"It's the dissoluteness of manners, Jacob, I'm sure you see it in your shop every day. There's a spirit of effeminacy, there is an intolerable share of pride and desire for luxury, and as for liquor, what did I tell you about that strong beer."

"Well vicar, I can't stop people buying what they wish."

"But you can stop it being sold in the first place."

"Hmm. Well, let me put it to you like this vicar. You tell us on a Sunday to help thy neighbour and to ensure that they have what they need." He looked slyly at the other." I believe that by providing the beer which they seek is part of God's way-"

"Now that is enough of that Jacob," said Joshua though not without a slight smile on his face. The man was, after all, only making available what was in demand. But the drinking was getting out of control. On Saturdays after ploughing the youth of the village would get hold of the beer by the clever ruse of getting their elder brothers to buy it and end up throwing their supper in the hedge to much raucous amusement.

"Talking of youth, vicar, I needs must go to Wetherby to obtain a licence. Molly intends to marry this Henry, young as they are."

"They are very young. I've not spoken with them yet. I need at least an hour with them together to let them see what they are taking on."

"Like me vicar. If I take a wife my costs drop overnight for I do not have to employ anyone to run my shop while I am in Wetherby for instance. As a bondsman my work is taking me more and more away from this main income. It is a costly business."

"Then you certainly should find a woman Jacob. Have you tried Thorp Arch?"

Jacob scowled. I'll not go near those people. There's something about them that makes me feel uncomfortable. They make me feel so...so down at heel. I know we are meant to be neighbours...and good neighbours and...Heavens, we all try...on both sides, but they *are* different from us in some way."

Chapter Ten

The Great Storm

Life, mused Edward Paul, vicar of St. Peter's in Walton was a strange mixture of positives and negatives. Fortune one day, poverty, or near to poverty, the next.

He was reading a diary of his predecessor, Joshua who had enjoyed his vicarage with its barn and outbuildings. At that time, the vicar would have had a good living. In the morning he would have arisen with the cockerel always to be found on Mrs. Potts' garden wall and walked the fifty yards or so to the church even as his choir were putting on their new, shortened versions of their surplices. But, by the end of Joshua's long life the vicarage was in such a state that Fairfax had declared it unsafe. Edward, on taking the job had been told by a rather sheepish sideman there was no accommodation in the village and he would have to travel from Thorp Arch on a daily basis. They had provided a good strong horse with massive fetlocks which sprouted long hair; judging by the size of the hoofs it was big enough to plough by, but at the end of the day it also meant more hay.

There were other benefits too, bestowed to keep him happy. A cask of strong beer, four times a year, and a cask of brandy every six months at the June Hay harvest, and at the ploughing in November.

There was also the need to keep the man from moving on for his title was only a stipendiary curate, or as officially described at the York office, a perpetual curate, a term Edward found rather amusing, as if he was going to endure life until Armageddon. Of course, in the village he was always addressed as 'Vicar' but there was always the continuing thought, lurking in the back of his mind the villagers might treat him with lesser respect than he was due.

His tithes, though, made him comfortable, of that he could not argue. Apples, cherries, walnuts and a whole range of other fruits assailed him in the Autumn. Calves, foals, geese in the spring and his bee hives grew under the care of his house-keeper. His problem became one of having to make up his mind on where to place himself during the day. His pastoral work required him to be in Walton while the delivery, say, of hay and clover, some rape and turnips required him to be at his barn to check them in correctly.

He sighed, then corrected himself as he realised how good his life had become and stooped as he walked out of the chancel door and down the slope to the south boundary wall. Masons in the village had been charged by Fairfax to repair the stonework for it was beginning to bulge and waver in parts with the load placed on it from the soil sliding down towards the road.

Christopher Hick touched his forelock as his vicar approached and turned to his men mixing lime in a wooden tub. Knowing Edward's attention to the finest detail, for the man's father had made a deal of money as a builder, he shouted out a command.

"Watch the lime lads. I don't want it in the vicar's eyes as he won't be able to see his sermon next Sunday."

Edward smiled. This was another reason for remaining here. It was just one big family of two hundred souls, all of whom he knew by name and occupation and a great deal besides and all of whom paid him two pennies at Easter. It was a most useful addition to his income.

"Mr. Hick, see that those joints are bedded in well. I notice some of the children try to pick out their initials every time they find new mortar to play with."

"We'll check it tonight, vicar but there's a storm coming, I can smell it in the air."

Edward looked up at the sky. "Do you think so, Mr. Hick?"

"Aye Vicar. The horizon is too clear for my liking. Bad one I reckon. I need to put some wet sacks over the wall to stop it drying out too quickly, and it will also protect it from the rain." He sent one of his apprentices off to search for some sacks from the cart and another to fetch more water from the nearby well. The last thing he needed was for the mortar to dry out too quickly.

A Tim Whisky, new in the village, drew up alongside, having come up from the Wetherby Road. It was Fairfax himself trying out his new one-horse carriage with its gleaming paintwork. The men fell back quickly to allow the keen eye to examine their work. "Satisfied Edward?" he called out as he reined in his horse which was eager to be away again. Its lips were dusted with oats.

"Good my Lord. This work will last a long time. It will see me out of here."

Mr. Hick was grateful for the comment. The vicar's support was valued. "Storm coming, my Lord. This evening I fear."

Fairfax acknowledged the advice as he touched his hat with his crop. The horse needed no further bidding and trotted off with its legs kicking high with each step. It reached the junction and turned left smoothly as it made for his Estate.

Edward turned back towards the church. He wanted to see if the new music sheets could be played. This man Handel had written a divine 'Messiah 'and it was the sort of music the whole village could participate in next Christmas. Such a show would cement the village as leading the region in its innovation even if winter was soon to begin to bite like iron into the cold houses.

He shivered as he felt a gust of wind blow up his cassock. Below him, the master mason was shouting instructions for his men to stop work and cover it up with the heavy sacking they had found. The sky had turned a dirty grey with smudges of yellow tinting the undersides to a sickly green. In the far distance, lightning lit up the darkened fields for seconds at a time. In the air lay the smell of ozone. Hick had been right. A storm was coming.

Rolling the music into a tight scroll in his saddlebag he swung a leg over his saddle and set off for his house anxious to check the security of his roofs and the barn doors. By the time he came down the Causeway into Thorp Arch the wind had begun to moan in the dead elm tree branches on Mrs. Pawson's land. Old leaves whipped up off the ground and blew dried manure from his yard to scour the cobbles so they looked as if they had been scrubbed with a broom. Unable to do anything more than retie his barn doors together with some stouter rope to prevent them clattering and banging themselves to destruction, he went indoors and gratefully took off his boots which had, of late, become too tight. Mrs. Harrison, his housekeeper met him, her hands clamped to her apron. Her hair was scraped back into a tight bun causing her face to look even more severe than he might like.

"I told Mrs. Pawson her tree is dangerous. It will come down one of these days, like in this wind if it continues to strengthen."

"Well, Mrs. Harrison, there's nothing we can do about it now. We are in God's hands."

His housekeeper sniffed slightly more loudly than was necessary to acknowledge his comment making it quite clear that God did not control the elements least of all the wind. She did not get on with her neighbour who had lived as a recluse for years. "A right lot of good that will do us vicar, if the tree comes down on my head and in my bed."

"Or poor Mrs. Pawson's head perhaps," said Edward wondering how long it would be before he was asked about supper.

Mrs Harrison's second sniff underlined her true feelings on the matter. It made it quite clear that a heavy elm branch landing on Mrs Pawson's head would finish the day off as nicely as one of her orange and apple puddings after roast beef but decided to hold her peace. "You have Mr. And Mrs. Horner coming to sup this evening, and Miss Chaucer. You will have your four for quadrille."

"Miss Chaucer is the only one of us who can score so it is just as well she has accepted. It is so infernally complicated and my mathematics is not as good as my history."

His housekeeper nodded her head fervently having had frequent run-ins with the vicar on totalling up his accounts.

"And what are we supping upon tonight, Mrs. Harrison?" There he had said it and he had promised himself he would keep it in check until asked. The problem was all because, despite the prickliness of the woman, she could cook like an angel.

"A dish of fish Sir, a leg of mutton, roasted, and some ham of course. I've made some of those small chicken tarts you like, the little ones with the cream in the sauce, peas in mint and roasted turnips. A syllabub to follow and some raspberry jellies." She studied his face cautiously, as she sought his approval.

"Excellent, excellent, Mrs. Harrison. You are the jewel in my household. Now, please stoke up the fire and I will prepare the table nearby for cards."

As he spoke, there came an enormous gust of wind which threw itself at the front door as if charged by a bull. He looked up in alarm. "If they come at all. This is a wild night and with no lights which will stay lit it will be a dark one."

All his housekeeper could think of was the food stacked up in her larder waiting to go into the ovens. But the two of them waited in vain for their visitors. The road quickly became impassable and a muddy boy, who had fallen over several times arrived later with a note. He had had to climb through the branches of a fallen tree to earn tuppence.

Edward was not unduly disappointed for he had had to go outside already to secure flying bales of hay and take them into the barn. On the ground lay strips of lead from his roof. As he paid the boy a further tuppence there came another huge gust followed by a long drawn out cracking, which seemingly rent open the earth itself. The crash, when it came awoke the whole village, those that were not still awake and in fear of their lives. Mrs. Harrison's half-wish to see Mrs. Pawson off this mortal world was granted a few seconds later as the main trunk sliced through her cottage. Asleep, abed without a worry, the lady never knew what hit her as the massive shaft forged a path through both floors of the house as if a knife heated in the fire was touched to butter.

The Great Storm blew with hail as large as broad beans rocking the houses in the village to their flimsy foundations. It howled and screamed out as if two devils were chasing each other across the countryside before coming to rest in the ruins of the cottage. Most residents lay with the bed sheets covering their heads, crying out to God to save them from the terrors of the night. It was only as dawn came into watery view that the wind collapsed into the willows down by the river and an eerie silence could be felt.

Broken tiles and thatch lay in the road the next morning along with tree branches, a bedstead from Mrs. Pawson's other bedroom and a dead donkey caught in a barn. Edward remembered the date of the storm for ever after for it was the day Walpole resigned from the Government. But, he knew the people of Walton would need him and he wanted to see how his church had fared. He munched on a cold chicken tart as he saddled up his horse.

He rode up the track and rounded the corner by the farm but found it difficult to find his bearings for a moment. Everywhere there was debris; large oak branches cracked through cleanly as though the work of an adze; someone's barn wall planking was distributed at random along the boundary wall of the church, piled as if they were bean sticks waiting for the farmer's wife to place them in rows. And the old vicarage, once a dilapidated ruin was now a pile of wattle and daub with the brick chimney standing forlornly as if it were a heron seeking an early meal of the day. Villagers were gathered around staring at the large south window of the chancel. A yew tree lay leaning tiredly against the wall although the stout stone tracery had prevented damage to all but the coloured glass installed by Sir John Fairfax which had gone. Small fragments lay scattered on the altar cloth. The watery sun battered by the storm illuminated piles of filth, dead leaves, dead birds and broken pans which had all been carried heavenwards before being forced through the gaps in the window and the main heavy south door. This had sprung its top hinge so it lay as if pushed aside by raiding Vikings. A roll of lead from the roof or the tower, of which Edward could not tell from this angle, had smashed a number of slates in its downward path.

"Anyone hurt?" was his first comment.

"Giles down at the Smithy, vicar. Caught a beam across his leg. Fair broke through I believe."

"Thanks be to God he was not killed."

"And Molly's prize sow has gone. Her pen was smashed and she has took off in a fright I reckon"

"We'll find her Jed. We'll put a party out. Now, who will help clear our church of Satan's work?"

There was a general murmur of agreement on both points. Edward removed his heavy riding coat and tethered his horse. "We will start with the nave and work our way forward. Be careful with the pulpit and the pews. They will all want a clean."

"Oh no vicar! Come and look at this."

"What is it Jed?" The voice had come from under the yew branches lying across the chancel.

"It's Fairfax, vicar. 'E's gorn and got damaged. It's 'is left leg and 'is sword, fair broke orf."

"Hmm, said Edward struggling through the greenery. "Lord Fairfax will not be best pleased with that." He held up a branch to let some more light fall on the effigy.

"There's his sword, or a bit of it."

But, although they found small pieces of the carved stone they could not be put back. Chips also had been knocked off the Knight as he slept, oblivious of the damage to himself.

It took the village the best part of the day to clear and clean the church. Lord Fairfax sent some of his men to help; big brawny men not often seen in the village. They spent much of their time ploughing and ditching though sometimes they turned up in the ale houses of Wetherby, of which there were dozens, on market day. The four lads soon had the heavy yew tree out of the window and some boards lashed across the opening. An hour later the blacksmith had made a new hinge for the south door and bolted it tightly as, with seemingly effortless ease the men lifted the door back on its pintles.

"All safe," said one, acknowledging the strong beer which had arrived at exactly the right time. The shop keeper was only too happy to distribute the drinks free of charge, and Molly's prize sow returned on its own none the worse for its adventure down the lane.

Edward could see that the church was secure and that there was no danger to his congregation but his wonderful glass was gone for good. Those pure reds and blues which no-one seemed able to make anymore, even if the village could afford to pay, would be missing from now on. He turned his mind to applying to the Church Commissioners for help with the repairs. He could see at least fifty pounds of damage and that was before they climbed up to the church roof, always a difficult task. The vertical steps had never been improved making it a risky business for the carpenter to make his annual visit.

The old church groaned to itself, creaking in dismay. The cleaners had always done such a good job; now the plaster was splattered with mud.

"We will have to worship in Thorp Arch until we have made repairs. If there is room," he pondered the space left on a Sunday. "That will bring the two villages together, of that I am sure. Four weeks of worship down the road and the next we will know is we will all be invited for a bite to sup."

"Steady on vicar. That may be too far," said one of the women, smiling nonetheless.

It did seem queer that his own parishioners would be coming to worship in the village where he took his rooms but, he also would have to seek permission to perform services for women himself. There was the need to bury Mrs. Pegg which might get in the way of Mrs. Pawson's relatives demands, if indeed there were any to be found. Death could put folk properly out of sorts if it was not carried out properly and according to all the rights developed over centuries.

He tipped his servant a shilling having seen how hard he had worked. The lad, barely seventeen, spotty in appearance but now filling out like a man should, wiped the sweat from his eyebrows.

"Thank you vicar, I'm much obliged to you Sir."

"You'll be less obliged after I have asked you to clear the debris down to that waiting cart." As a workman's wages was about two shillings a day the lad felt he had done pretty well out of his work.

"I'll start now vicar, and we'll be done by nightfall."

Edward turned to the gathered tradesmen all eager for the work. He needed to have the best price for their trades in turn. The list lengthened as the roofer, carpenter, mason, plasterer and the painter added to the total.

"Tell you what, vicar. Why don't we have a ploughing competition...to raise money that is? We charge people to enter, or just to watch and have some fun at the same time...music...dancing...bit of ale...make a day of it."

It was a good idea for there was no guarantee the Church Commissioners would come up with any help. Fairfax himself would have to be involved and perhaps he could underwrite the loan. The problem was the Lord of the Manor was at that present time knocking his own home down in order that he could build a better, larger house. A great deal of time and money was being channelled into the project and Edward could not see a great deal of enthusiasm for two building schemes running together. However, the church belonged to Fairfax and it would be his reputation at stake if he did nothing while he made his own house more comfortable.

Edward was surprised, therefore, when he received a welcome visitor that summer with news that the damage would be met in full, albeit without replacing the coloured glass in the south wall of the chancel. The ploughing competition, which had raised the amazing sum of fifty-six pounds and tu'pence, was channelled into funds set up to rebuild the vicarage in the future. The Church Commissioners:

'...*were not able at that time to do anything with regard to his accommodation and could not help with regard to replacing the valued coloured glass but we feel that with clear glass it will let the Lord's light in and brighten the interior,*' not a particularly helpful comment but one he could not argue with. Edward, as he saw it, would have to remain where he was in Thorp Arch for the time being.

*   *   *   *   *

While the damage of the Great Storm was made good and the debris carted off as fire wood, the shop had continued to expand, not only in what it sold and produced itself but in the types of service it dispensed. John Bagthorpe had taken over; marrying into the village which, as well as a bride, came a shop. The building had fallen into some disrepair over the past few years and it took the young couple a full year before they could see their hard work begin to pay dividends.

Widow Elena was in the shop that afternoon when the news came in that Captain Cook had been killed by savages on the far side of the world. It caused quite a stir in the village for the Captain had hailed from Whitby not two days coach travel from the village well. And of travel the other news to make the widow shake her head in amazement and wonder at things modern was the billboard pinned to the shop door informing all and sundry that a regular mail coach would operate into Wetherby from then on.

"Being a mail coach means it will be faster to get to Leeds-"

"Or London," broke in John excitedly. "Takes four inside and a guard on the back."

"Guard the mail, whatever for? It's going nowhere without the driver."

"He will see the mail is not stolen on the way Elena. And this is going to put Wetherby on the map, and it should become a regular stopping off point. There are forty inns already in the town. Seems," his eyes narrowed at the thought, "seems I should set up another shop over there...for the daytime, of course."

Widow Elena pulled the shawl tighter to her shoulders as she gazed at the man who never wanted to rest for a moment in the day. It was, and always had been a problem for Mary his wife to get him to church on a Sunday for although the shop was closed her husband always found need to arrange a funeral, or a baptism, or taking his seat on the village council to deal with passing vagrants and rowdy itinerants. Waltonians wanted to be reassured that whenever rough looking men with no real reason to be in their particular part of the country were passing by they were seen to the boundary road leading on to the town. They never had any money for the shop and they certainly were not going to church.

But most of all, John wanted land. He could see the risk to buy land was minimal for the price rose every year and if he didn't buy soon, it would be too expensive to get even a vegetable patch of ground.

He was in a better position than most for one of his duties he had taken on was as the auctioneer on all property sales, most of which, these days was for land. It was his job to light the candle and to monitor the bids until the candle snuffed out whence he would declare the sale was valid and firm. He was able to time the call by the dying flickers of the candle to the second: he only needed ready cash to make a fortune, go up in the world, be someone at last.

He suddenly remembered his duty and why he was there. "Widow Elena. You need something else?" She was eyeing the rows of bottles of gin. Free of licence still, it appeared as if half of the village drank to some degree or other of the colourless liquid, distilled from juniper. Men had their ale; women had their gin and they had begun to drink it in increasing quantities.

But Elena wasn't buying. "A dozen of your herring's Master John if you please, and my maid needs a new pair of clogs. She is down to the last quarter inch," she paused glancing around carefully. "Those bread puddings: did Mary make them herself?"

"Aye, she did that. She's good at cooking, my Mary."

Alas, there was one thing Mary could not do, and that was to produce an heir, someone who would be able to take over the shop or shops when they were wanting to sit in the sun or arranging flowers in the church. John believed it was just a matter of time, but the truth was as much that he was so tired at night he would collapse into bed into a deep sleep. With Mary abroad at first light collecting eggs and milking the cows the matter of producing a baby rather than pullets or heifers was constantly being set aside.

"The vicar's putting on his spring fête as usual, come Michaelmas. Will you be running your ribbon stall again this year?"

Elena pursed her lips, unsure what to say and certainly unsure what to do. On the one hand she had been making ribbons for as long as she could remember. There wasn't a woman in the village or down in Thorp Arch who didn't have one or more of her ribbons; even the prize bulls wore her rosettes. But new ribbons were arriving in Wetherby from over the Dales. There was news of machines capable of producing yards and yards of ribbon in a day, and so cheaply she could not compete on price any longer and she could not imagine where her income would come from in the future, which darkened her life with a new fear. If it had only been ribbons, the village might have been able to pull together as it always had, helping one another through bad times. But these machines were springing up like dawn mushrooms, not only to make ribbons but to make farming equipment, equipment to mine coal and others to carry coal to the waiting ships, while all the time the stuff of war was improved beyond all recognition.

Now men could kill other men with considerable ease while they sat back and watched their new explosive destroy rank after rank of the enemy. Rifles became more accurate. From ribbons to rifles, each and every new design meant less work for men whether he be a ploughboy or a candlestick maker.

"This will be my last year," she concluded at last. "I'll see how it goes and if no-one needs my work then it is God's plan for me to do something else." The placidity of her soul had always been a comfort to the villagers. Nothing ever altered her view on the world however disastrous it appeared from time to time. Her belief in the church and what it stood for was as solid as the foundations on which St. Peters stood.

"You heard about the King, God bless him?" John asked suddenly, reminded of a conversation he had had the day previous.

"What news is that then?" Widow Elena still eyed the herrings to see they were the larger ones going into her bag.

"They say he is as mad as a hatter. They say he is having to have treatment privately, without anyone knowing, as it were, though, for heaven's sake, we know about it so most of the world must also know."

"Mad? I ain't 'eard 'bout that. That's awful if it is true."

"I hear they have brought in a special man, used to dealing with these cases."

"But, what can any doctor do? They give you potions and lotions but none of them seems to make you better. Old Mrs Yardley, up on the corner, she's just as good, going out into the fields, picking them 'erbs from the 'edges. I always takes 'er remedies."

"Well, I can't think the King would use any of Mrs Yardley's potions because she isn't grand enough for him."

"Then, we shall have a mad King to rule us tho' I doesn't think it makes any difference up 'ere, does it?"

"I don't suppose it does, Widow Elena. Now, anything else?" The vicar was coming along the road again and he needed a word. Perhaps the vicar could put in a good word for him at the Hall regarding the piece of land along the east road to York. It could take a number of houses and was close to the Smithy and money was there to be made in property these days for sure. It was just a matter of getting hold of the land, then building one at a time: house by house as the demand showed its face in the colour of money. And then he needed to get over to Wetherby to see where a shop could be built catering for the travellers as they stopped overnight.

Mary popped her head in to see if he was busy. "What's for tonight dear?"

"A pig's face and an apple pudding if you are good," she replied with a smile. John loved his food and it was beginning to show on his stomach in sharp contrast to some less well-off in the village. Widow Elena nodded briefly as she left the shop preferring male company to that of the women.

Chapter Eleven

We All Stray from Time to Time

James Rudd was one of those people who found it difficult to delegate. Being the vicar of Walton meant that he often came into conflict with those that deemed it their duty to help out, whether it be the cleaning, organising the fetes or arranging the hedge flowers in jars. As he failed to entrust many to his plans, he also failed to let them know when important events were coming into the calendar. This caused upsets, tears from the ladies and many saucers of tea which had to be administered with a soothing voice as a result. It was not that he did it deliberately and was genuinely remorseful when something went wrong but his head was into so many others things than organising the rota for the women to wash his shirts.

The problem assailing his mind today was the continuing fighting and arguments landing firmly on his doorstep every time there was a football match in the village. He was not sure if it was the disposition of the teams, being as they usually were, split between married men and the bachelors. This in itself was not a problem and gave rise to much ribaldry as they lined up for the start. The trouble arose again that day wherein the bachelors had *run amuck* and were thrashing the married men, some say 9-2. Disappointed at being made a laughing stock in the village the married men reacted badly as they lost their control and began to lash out as the game drew towards the last few minutes. Badly grazed shins, broken noses and a cracked rib led to calls of foul play not being hurled at the referee but to the vicar who was usually to be found on the edge of the field. Not satisfied with the adjudication, one of the wives, having dressed her husband's wounds, entered the fray and began to dribble the ball expertly towards the net. The bachelors, confounded at first by the sight of a long dress on the muddy field shouted for her to leave – or words to that effect – but she carried on gamely and sent the ball, with some considerable skill and force between the flailing arms of the opposition goal keeper and on into the stinging nettles. A great cheer went up which turned to roars of rage when the referee agreed it was an acceptable goal.

"Vicar! Vicar! Did you see that?" The bachelors cried out which seemed pointless as they had won the game anyway. Behind James Rudd's back the woman in question made a rather pointed signal at the opposition's captain and wiped her shoes of most of the mud. James smiled behind his hat not wishing to take sides in this most important game where twenty guineas were at stake. He, after all, had to hand out the prize money to the winners.

James withdrew from the fray and walked back to the gathering of villagers as he waved away the grumbles. "It was a fair fight, er game...in the end...and the bachelors won quite clearly despite some issues."

He recalled to mind another fight as uneven as this one. It had been a hundred years earlier, so the stories went in the bar, when William Nevison had been found sleeping under a tree one warm summer evening rather like this one. Nevison had a reputation as a Highwayman and had once galloped his mare Black Bess from London to York to provide himself with an alibi. On finding the recumbent thief snoring his head off the villagers had rallied the men with pitchforks and any other tool they could lay their hands upon. On being touched on the shoulder by one of the breathless group Nevison had woken to find himself surrounded by an assemblage of would-be policemen. He jumped up and pulled a branch of elderberry roughly shaped like a gun. Immediately and without further thought the men charged off towards their homes without looking back. Their wives had been angry with them then for not collecting the reward and, unfortunately for Walton, the event had been recorded, not without some smirks, in the local newspaper. The village had hoped the incident would be forgotten over the years but there would always be some wag coming up from the south who had heard the story in a coaching inn where he had stopped over for the night. Nevison paid for his thievery and was hanged though not without some admiration for the man who had acted as a latter day Robin Hood of Yorkshire from time to time.

If he was completely honest with himself, James knew it was not the football match that tickled away at his mind, where concerns lodged easily with his character. He was determined to do better for the village, to increase attendances, improve the quality of the services and to remind everyone of their duties to the church. The dilemma was, this time, and it was becoming a very visible problem, the conversion of the end room in Walnut Tree cottage into a meeting room for the Wesleyan Methodist church and its growing number of attendees. To a number of Waltonians James's ardour for the true word was becoming a yoke around their necks. In these modern days the people were not obliged to attend the church at all though they might find it hard at times if they completely ignored the requests from the vicar. Here, immediately opposite the church, almost as if an engineer had measured it so, stood the meeting room of these strange people who changed the word from High to Low Church without warning. Their 'love feasts and camp meetings' were, to say the least he felt, dangerous and departed from everything that the people of this great nation had been brought up to believe. There were a few good ideas: intemperance not being tolerated was one and the abolition of slavery, certainly a second. But if the people felt so strongly about these matters why had they not brought them to the attention of the clergy who might have reacted positively to the requests. Or, would they, he mused?

Sometimes people began to believe more and more strongly that the clergy, the vicars themselves were so 'high-minded' so out of touch with the day to day lives of the congregations they served that their pleas would never be heard let alone accepted.

Now, these new clergy had gone and rented a room in Walnut Tree farm just where the idea of a school room had been planned. This was a far more dangerous situation than James liked to think, for if these Methodists managed to combine their teachings with those of the education authorities the sect would spread like a virulent disease and there could be far worse effects than the plague of so many years earlier.

That Sunday, James stood up in his pulpit and addressed his full church. He gazed down on bonnets and shawls and the bare heads of the men allowing a full minute to pass before he spoke. It had its effect and brought attention to his cause.

"Friends. We all stray from time to time. Often we do not know why we need the greener grass on the other side of the road, other than it looks better than that which we enjoy on this side. When we have a grumble, when our pastor does not act in accordance with the wishes of the parishioner, we often keep it within ourselves where it turns to vinegar and the sourness spreads across the dining table.

Across the road is a group of people, most from this village of ours, who decided that as they cannot take their grumbles to the vicar, because, perhaps they have no backbone or are simply afraid to raise their problem, they would throw off the cloak of Anglicanism as easily as they might cast off their winter coat at the end of May. It is so easy for the preacher in Walnut Farm to agree with all of his converts' wishes," he began to thump the top of the lectern to emphasize his points," but, in the end they get no further, they find no further solace, no dream fulfilled and they begin to look enviously back across our road and up the green hill to St. Peter's. The plain, drab form of service is really not for them, the promises not kept because most of these are government promises and not ecclesiastical ones yet they find they cannot cross this enormous gulf which had been our road until recently, back to our side because of the fear of ridicule. Ridicule! We, here in our church will never laugh or make fun of our neighbours just because they have made a mistake. We here in our church will welcome them back just as that father so long ago welcomed his own son back into his house.

So, I ask you all to speak to these neighbours of yours, of ours, and say that they are welcome back here beside you any time they wish. All they have to do is to walk up the path and sit down and listen to the way which has been preached for hundreds of years.

There was considerable shuffling of feet behind the wooden pews. John Smythe was already considering crossing the road, after he had had a drink or two though he had been warned he would have to watch his drinking in future if he was to convert to the Wesleyans. Most of the ladies looked on demurely confident in their attire and their thoughts on the summer strawberry festival and of Miss Jurgens's state of mind for she had been seen wandering the road late at night calling out to a group of owls. The village would need to start thinking of caring for her soon as it was unlikely she would be allowed to continue for much longer unaided. Her state of undress at the time of these nocturnal walks was also something of considerable concern to the Parochial Church committee.

James, casting his eye wide to the back of the church saw fidget, disinterest and a wish to be out of the service at which time the men could get down to the Black Bull before lunch. He sighed inwardly. When Lord Nelson had died fifteen years earlier there had been a great upwelling of patriotism in the entire country. The Government felt they were in control and the people certainly, were kindly disposed towards one another. If only he could invoke just a small fraction of that well-being now.

"And John," he ended looking down on the man who he knew was dallying with the idea of joining up with the opposition, "not too much drinking before lunch."

Chapter Twelve

'Owd Jimmy

James Fox-Lane, known to all his huge circle of friends as 'Owd Jimmy pursed his lips in annoyance while drumming his manicured hands on the polished top of his bureau. He was a gentle man in so many ways and with an enormous capacity for kindness and, one might say, so he could with the wealth of Croesus, but his help often went deeper and unnoticed. He was, his wife knew, a modest man, disliking the bright lights of London and the Court and the eternal round of visiting other families in their country houses.

Jimmy preferred above all else in life to kill: foxes, rabbits, pheasants, woodcock, snipe and deer, the list seemed endless as it spanned the seasons. If it moved he would shoot it, providing there was no seasonal edict as to why the animal should not be shot. So long as there was something to shoot at or to ride at Jimmy was never happier, where he could leave the problems of the Estate and his family to one side for a few hours of pleasure. All would be forgotten until the last fence when he would climb down stiffly from his saddle and return in the late afternoon to the issues of the day.

His problem now, lay in his son, George. James had worked very hard all of his life to restore the family fortunes and they were now greater than they had ever been even in the height of the glory days save for the fact his son was spending it as quickly as it was earned.

"Godamnit George! I've bailed you out three times...and for what? For your gambling and you are not even good at that-"

"But father, I disagr-"

"Quiet when your father is talking to you!" The voice cut like a coachman's whip around the book-lined walls of the study. "Do you realise that your gambling, your drinking and your whoring are doing to this family?"

George, whose hand had been creeping towards a cut-glass decanter of port to where he had positioned himself earlier in the full knowledge he was going to be grilled, now checked his move.

"Twice...twice you have promised me you will stop, grow up and become a man. Twice you have broken your promise as if you were a lowly form of worker in a factory and not a man of the landed gentry. Can you give me a single reason why I should pay them off this time?"

"Well," said George, seeing an opportunity to regain the high ground. "If I go to prison for not paying my debts it is your name that will be dragged through the mire. The Prime Minister will-"

"The Prime Minister. Yes indeed, William Pitt. Do you know what I have turned down? Do you?" The usually quiet man's eyes blazed up as if someone had thrown a log onto the fire.

"No father, but no doubt you are going to tell me," came the insolent reply. For a moment in time it looked as if George had gone too far. Then his father sank backs on his heels before slumping down into a chair. "I turned down the offer, freely given by Mr. Pitt to reinstate the peerage of Bingley...that is what I did."

George's face collapsed as a cod's will do when it is finally hauled up on a trawler's deck. "But, but that means you have taken away the peerage which would have come to me eventually."

"What we never had, son, we will never miss."

George, however, bit his lip in anguish so it bled. Comfortable in the company of the Prince Regent he would, nonetheless have been able to make further inroads into the highest levels of society if he could have become a peer of the realm. It was so unfair.

"You've done this deliberately, father, just to spite me. Now, you will die an ordinary man just to get your own back."

James smiled. "I doubt it son, but I'm a modest man in life and am not seeking greatness for the sake of it and, despite your cruel words, after all the times I have bailed you out from going to a debtor's prison, it is quite untrue. I merely wish to remain a humble man."

George could contain himself any longer. "That's good. That's really ripe. A humble man? A modest man you say, yet, last Sunday you turn up at that little church in Walton in a coach and four...and...an outrider to boot."

"I am expected to travel in the way people regard me son."

His son, however, could not hold back his need for the ruby-red stickiness of the port glinting in the shaft of light entering the window. He pulled off the stopper and poured himself a measure, then doubled it.

"Look at you son. Nineteen stones, nanny tells me; you cannot walk because your gout is so bad. What on God's earth do you see when you look into a mirror in the morning?"

But George now realised there was little point in reminding his father of the new debt. As his father had not mentioned it again he could safely assume it would be paid, distasteful as the whole matter was. He thought of London beckoning with a renewed line of credit. He choked back his violent temper he was famous for and attempted to placate his father.

"It is not my fault father. It's Georgiana's. She spends all of our money as if she owned the Royal Mint."

This was partly true. James was well aware of his son's wife's profligacy and her expensive salons which she steadfastly refused to give up."You cannot hide behind her anymore lad. Besides, I have now made a decision. I am not expected to live that much longer, in the average of things I may last another three or four years. I have decided that when I am dead I do not want the family name to be tainted with what I am sure will be further, appalling expenditure as you work your way through my assets. I have worked all of my life to build this Estate only to find that after my death it will be turned very probably into a whorehouse and casino."

"So, what are you planning father?"

"I am changing my name, George so that when I die I will die with some honour."

George paled visibly. The name was of considerable value to him in London. It meant something to the bookies." But-"

"No 'buts' George. From now on I will be known as Lane-Fox. Some will realise the change is for a reason, others will notice it as a split in the family; other again will probably not notice any different. After all I changed my name by Act of Parliament once; now I am changing it again. The real facts are son that you will have to make your own way in the world and, with a new name to make public, which, God willing, will cause the people to look up to in the future?"

"But, meanwhile?"

"Meanwhile son I intend to pay off some of your debts, but not all. You are going to have to work for a change which means staying here. I want to buy Walton and you can help me."

"But, why Walton?"

"Very good farming land, George, close to the estate and you are going to help me all the way to get it."

"But, I am due in London tomorrow."

Not any longer, you are not. Either you stay here and work or I do not clear your debts, which means you cannot go to London anyway."

"But, the Prince-"

"Sorry son. That's the end of it."

George swallowed the port in one frustrated gulp and stormed from the room. James, seeing his left hand shaking slightly stared out of the window at the Estate grounds. Gradually he calmed down as he began to consider how Walton would fit into his plans in the future.

Chapter Thirteen

Mrs Yorke

Thomas Wilson, stooped and gnarled as if he was a bunch of roots emerging from the base of an oak tree looked up with his ice-blue eyes now faded to duck-egg milk. His chest was full of phlegm which made his sermons the more difficult to listen to while his chest wheezed and hummed between each word and the sentences ended in a sort of dying gasp. This would, inevitably cause his congregation to look up from where they been studying the floor anxiously, wondering if their vicar was living his last day on earth. Thomas had lived in the village most of his life and understood the weaknesses, and strengths of every one of his parishioners. With four shoe makers, a very capable wheelwright across the road, Sam the tailor and eight farms to come to terms with each Sunday he was always busy travelling the breadth of the village from the east end of Hall Park Road past St. Helens Wishing Well and up to Goosemoor Lane before reversing the whole thing before nightfall. He knew he needed to read the Riot Act to them about the two inns where just lately there had been far too much carousing and, as they were at opposite ends of the village to each other, the drunken youths would be found walking from one to the other seeking their friends in the noisiest way.

England was changing rapidly, he knew; Yorkshire also and he had to remain on top of the disharmony which threatened to colour the village if he and his church wardens did not keep a very firm lid on the pot.

His immediate need was to agree with James Lane-Fox, a Captain in the Army, the provision of land to build a school on the west end of the village. After the cramped conditions in Walnut Tree Farm, the very room where the Wesleyan Methodists had held their services, the village needed more space to accommodate their children. But, he had to be careful. Her Majesty's Inspector's of Schools was very clear on what a school should be, on what it should provide and what the children could expect, let alone their anxious parents seeking a better education than themselves. And, with cholera on the move throughout the country the school had to be careful in keeping the invisible miasmas out of the buildings. So far, Thomas believed there was some sort of connection with fresh air and the healthy living of the villagers which had kept this dread disease away, but it only needed one small thing to go wrong, say with the well, and half the population would be lost.

As well as keeping the Education Inspectors happy the village had been asked to contribute towards the Afghan War breaking out almost, it seemed, on the other side of the world, where the Opium Wars was yet another issue muddling the Government's plans. But, England had another Queen on the throne, a tough woman who already reflected some of the strengths that had been seen three hundred years earlier.

"We need a plan," said Thomas to his housekeeper that afternoon after he had spoken to the shopkeepers who helped administer the church. "We need a plan so we do not sink under the weight of all of this legislation we are forced to listen to."

"Yes Vicar," said Nellie. She was used to the vicar speaking out aloud, seemingly to her, but in reality merely giving vent to his frustrations in his failing strengths.

"What sort of plan do you er...plan Vicar?"

"We need to see everyone is involved in this school. At least, all parents so there are no arguments in the future that we have left something out."

"But, something might be expensive, more expensive than we can afford Vicar. Then where will we be?"

"I have a belief that Lane-Fox will see us through this one, Nellie. After all, if it goes wrong he will be tainted with the same tar as me."

"How much is such a school going to cost Sir?"

"Maybe two hundred pounds... or more."

Nellie blew air out of her mouth. "Then it's just as well harvest time is coming up. We are all going to need that extra bit of pocket money."

James well understood that harvest time was a season when the locals could make some useful extra income. The idea of them having to put it into the school seemed hard and he stiffened his belief that Lane-Fox had to come up with all of the necessary funds.

"What about Mrs Yorke, of Wighill Park, Vicar? She has always wanted to help out with education for children. She could afford to pay for a school completely."

"Well, maybe not all," replied Thomas though attracted immediately to the idea. Mrs Yorke was one of those 'do-gooders' who accomplished whatever she set out to do. Mrs Yorke was a veritable champion of the depressed and the forgotten and might well take an interest in his proposals.

"An excellent idea, Nellie, if I may so. I shall go and see her this very afternoon."

And, Thomas, being Thomas, following a good lunch, climbed up the steps to his horse and sat astride painfully. As his legs widened and the hip sockets ground against very little cartilage, he mused on how long he could go on riding. This new steam engine which had arrived in Wetherby might well be his form of transport in the future though the idea of getting into one of those small wooden coaches and lurching along at frightening speeds was not something he would look forward to, say, as fishing might be.

Mrs Yorke received the vicar on the porch outside her greenhouse, more of a palm court than a place to grow those tomatoes which everyone was talking about. The glass was formed into a lean-to with ornate cast-iron swirls as supports.

"My dear Vicar," she exclaimed as he was announced. "What a pleasant surprise to see a man I have admired for so many years. Please, sit down," she said, seeing the man was almost literally creaking with age.

Thomas eased himself into a comfortable cushioned rattan cane chair and gazed around at the lush planting. The air was heady with scents not one of which he recognised. Something looking like a bunch of very green bananas hung not far from his left ear.

"Tea?"

"That would be very kind of you, Mrs. Yorke."

They made inconsequential talk until a silver tray arrived with a set of exquisite porcelain cups. As she poured she enquired after the reason for his visit for she could see he had ridden all the way from Walton on a bony horse.

"Mrs. Yorke, I am a plain speaking man and I would like to come straight to the point. Walton needs a school and needs it very soon. The numbers of children are increasing-"

"Forgive me vicar, how many children do you have of school age?"

"Sixteen Mrs Yorke, but there are also children of course away across the fields in Wighill here, and Thorp Arch."

Mrs. Yorke's eyes gleamed as she saw images which her visitor clearly had not. "So what size school were you considering...to build I assume?"

She was at least initially on side and understanding his initial proposal. "We have in mind a schoolroom for sixty children, possibly eighty scholars in total with a library of, say, one thousand volumes to be available also to the people of

Walton on a borrowing basis. One teacher and an assistant to begin with, an office and an earth closet out the back. If we could have enough land in the front of the building we could have physical training."

As he spoke, Thomas's face became more and more aroused with a passion not seen in him for twenty years. Wighill's gracious incumbent was not slow to catch the mood.

"How would they sit?"

There would be separate classes set on three sides, good desks and chairs and a well-equipped office for the head master. There! That's the plan in its basic form."

"And, you would like me to put some money into the construction."

The word 'construction' was quite a grand one for a building of the size Thomas envisaged but it sent the right message.

"Yes please, very much so."

"Do you have any funding yet?"

"No, ma'am."

"So, if I were to inject some capital others might follow?"

"It is my belief that Lane-Fox will follow almost immediately...not to be caught out so to speak Mrs. Yorke. He is, I believe, sometimes slow on the uptake but always catches up very fast."

"The dear man was injured very badly, as you know, in that hunting fall which has slowed him down tremendously, but his heart is there and I am sure that between us we could find the money. About two hundred pounds I think?"

Thomas was astounded by the breadth of the woman, her understanding and her ability to ease the difficult problem forward. "Well, yes, but it would be nice to have a contingency." Was he pushing his luck too far?

"Perhaps this is where the village could contribute?"

"Yes, of course." She had a point.

"I want you to send me the plans. Get your builder, or do you have an Architect to send a copy to James, and I will call on him to obtain his co-operation."

Dear old Nellie. Without her simple advice clearly seen, he might never have got this far so quickly. Within a year there might be a school in the village and one built for the purpose. Thomas rose slowly to take his leave, brushing against exotic flowers on the way. In the background, he could see two journeymen weeding the gravelled path and another feeding a carrot to his horse which was waiting patiently under the shade of a chestnut tree.

"I cannot thank you enough Mrs Yorke. The village will be so..." he stopped for the moment overwhelmed with what he had achieved. With so few years left to do what he had set out to achieve, this would be a lasting monument to his life's work. His rheumy eyes misted over. Mrs Yorke became embarrassed.

"Come and see me again Vicar. This has been a very pleasant sojourn, very pleasant indeed."

Thomas set off down the road, his horse well able to get him home without the twitch of a rein as a thousand thoughts crossed his mind. Who could he find as a head master? And the books? Who would choose those and buy them? He would need catalogues and advice; and he needed to make a visit to Lane-Fox very soon...allowing a decent time before Mrs Yorke had also made her visit to Bramham Park. He would need the land before he had even considered a builder for the work.

That evening Nellie set down one of his favourite dishes of bubble and squeak with cold veal. Her pickles were known throughout the village which he spooned out with a sigh of delight, happy with the events of the day and enjoying the benefits of his office.

Chapter Fourteen

Her Majesty's Inspectors

"But, who are they?" Miss Smith wanted to know. She did not like any interruptions whatsoever during the course of the school day, yet here were three well-dressed people, two ladies and a gentleman, asking, almost demanding to have entry. She quietened the room and stepped through the door into the small lobby where the coats and hats were hung. Her assistant, Miss Goodbody stepped tactfully aside.

"Miss Smith? We are the Inspectors from Her Majesty's Inspectors of schools. We are charged with inspecting every school to ensure that the curriculum is as we set down in the Committee of Council on Education."

Miss Smith shook hands. "You do realise that the children are here, already engaged for the day in arithmetic?"

"Quite so, Miss Smith, but that is exactly the reason why we have come at this time. We need to see the children at work."

"And at play," said the man who had not introduced himself. "They do play, we assume?"

"Absolutely. Every morning before they begin their day they are out here in front of you doing a series of exercises to let them receive God's air into their lungs. It freshens them up, clears their eyes, essential to their well-being. And... some of them need it more than others," she ended, her face changing sombrely. She was only too aware of the five children she had who were likely not to have had any breakfast before setting out across the fields to school. She kept a large tin of biscuits on a shelf in her office for such events and would call them in one at a time to allow them to select one or more of the delectable goodies. We do forward bends, arm circles, skipping, the boys do tug-of-war."

"Very good. May we go in?"

Miss Smith stood aside to allow the three arrivals to enter the room. The ceiling soared to the roof with strong stone walls covered in pictures. Lancet windows reminiscent of an early church permitted the room to be flooded with light. There was a map of the world mostly coloured in pink showing the limits of the British Empire and a diagram of a frog which had been dissected. On the opposite side was a screened-off office. Light was pouring in all directions. As the party entered the classroom, the children, all twenty-six of them, rose as one and stood quietly until told to sit down. The three inspectors smiled to reassure the children they were not going to be beaten with a ruler that day and spent some time looking at the work on the walls. Then they transferred their attention to Miss Smith's office and were pleased to note the rows and rows of books, all neatly labelled. Outside too, they walked and the man poked his head into the earth closet which had a pile of carefully torn up newspapers on a string.

"Excellent," said the elder of the three, or at least the woman who had shown command of her small group. "Excellent in tone and order. The only item we find to be queried is the attendance record for last winter."

"That," replied Miss Smith very quickly, "was due to the severity of the winter. You may remember that we had drifts six feet deep for many weeks and the children were unable to get here. Even I had to struggle to make the front door and men in the village had to dig a passageway from School Lane as we now call it. We have also had sickness in a number of families when the children have had to look after their mother or another child"

"Quite so," the leader replied recalling reading in the newspapers of the weather that had played havoc in the north. "In my opinion, and having seen many schools, there is no place where more earnest and intelligent efforts have been made for the sound education of the working people."

"Quite so, and thank you," Miss Smith did not like the inference made towards the poorer classes in the village even if the facts were plain for all to see. Nonetheless she was pleased someone had recognised her efforts and those of the vicar, Thomas.

As for the vicar, the creation of his school had had a remarkable effect on him. Remaining bent and crooked so he now had to look upwards to all but the youngest of children with his back almost horizontal to the ground he had managed to live through the repeal of the Corn Laws, the cholera epidemic and the coming of steam power. Hardly a week went by these days without some new invention appeared in the local newspaper, or in a catalogue or sometimes to be seen trundling down the main street towards Walton Hall. And these days he would receive two shillings and sixpence for a marriage and a further two shillings to bury the family later. The living was good clouded only by the difficulties the Bramham Estate was putting upon Walton with regard to a Parsonage.

It had started off well, with George Lane-Fox offering land to be made available for a Parsonage of three rods and twenty-five perches, more than enough to satisfy any vicar and fifty pounds towards its construction. Then, it had all turned sour with the Ecclesiastical Commissioners becoming involved. Perhaps they had been greedy, demanding more than the patron was prepared to provide but in the end George had withdrawn the offer and the issue of a parsonage continued on into the century as it had for a hundred years or more before. Lunching with Lane-Fox at the estate one Sunday, Thomas had broached the sensitive subject of a vicarage, somewhere where he could have a permanent base and one that the village would also recognise as his proper home. By this time he had served the community for twenty-four years and he felt the Commissioners should by now have recognised his worth.

"My dear vicar. If I could do more, I would be only too pleased to be involved. But letters have been going back and forth to York for three years now and I really cannot spend any more time on the subject. The trouble is, those fat rascals over in York are just not interested in anything outside their own tiny bailiwick."

While Thomas privately agreed with the Lord's comments he was hardly able to confirm approval of them. "But sire, they are busy men-"

"Pah, Thomas! I doubt if one in three of them would be able to point out Walton on a map if asked to do so. No, I am sorry but until these clerics make some promises, and on paper too I can do nothing more. The Estate just does not allow it even if I wanted to."

This was nonsense, the vicar knew, for if Lane-Fox had opened his mouth on any subject at all he would have had immediate attention. It was becoming clear that one or more of the ecclesiastics in York had upset the manor or his Estate Manager.

"Meanwhile, perforce, I must reside in my house which has the name, Fox Cottage but not vicarage."

George Lane-Fox took a draft of port and turned to other affairs. "There must be something in the water, the well in Walton. I have been given the ages of all residents in the village and you would seem to have at least three parishioners over ninety years of age and one over a hundred years old. Can this really be true?"

"Yes Sire, indeed this is true. Whether it is the water or the fresh air I know not but the village gets older each year. I myself am approaching seventy-four."

"Are you really? And you still ride?"

"Yes, but not to Hounds of course. The village is growing in size and my work takes most of each day. With Wetherby connected to Leeds and York by this railway and the stage coach running several times a day, more and more people are coming to live in the area. It's good farming land."

"I know that Thomas. I see the results each month from my manager. By the way, I am reliably informed that the authorities in York under which you take notices, is to declare Walton a vicarage very soon."

"Praise be the Lord. That has only taken five hundred years to do. But, it is important, for it recognises, at long last, my role and the church's role in the village."

George looked at the vicar over the rim of his glass, seeing the old man's face suddenly glow with delight. He had been meaning to tell him for a couple of weeks but the season was on him and most other things had turned out to be more important.

He began to realise what he had said. Walton had never been declared a 'true' vicarage even if it acted as if it were one. It had retained this title of a perpetual curacy for as long as there were records and the implication of the term perpetual was not missed on him. As he was well reminded there was not even a vicarage to live in despite five hundred years of service to the people of Walton. He pondered upon whom in York had continually dismissed the idea of bringing this particular village into the fold. A good lunch, perhaps? A nod and a comment from someone well-placed, and one who bore a grudge against perchance himself.

He felt guilty all at once. Surely it was part of his role in life to impact the good people who served him so well and who worked within his estates? He had to demonstrate he could lead in such matters.

"I'll speak again with York. Perhaps now, being a vicarage they will understand you need your own house, something of stature, somewhere for you to entertain."

With each word George felt better in himself. The constant pain from his hunting accident eased as he realised he could win over many of the parishioners who had begun to lose faith in him since he had had to stop many of his day to day outings around his Estate.

Thomas smiled inwardly, for God, he believed, had also smiled down on him.

Agnes Goodall, a gentlewoman in every respect invited to the meal for her intelligent conversation and widespread travel stories in Europe nodded in confirmation. She was dressed entirely in grey as if underlining a subdued statement of sobriety in all things English.

"This would be such a good thing for you to do, George. Thomas deserves his house more than most, what with his school work and his church, always full on a Sunday."

George Lane-Fox gazed through the window of the dining room, past the heads of the ten guests and, not for the first time in many years, came to understand how lucky he was. By an accident of birth, no more or less, he was able to say that he owned all of the land in sight and beyond to Walton. But for a trick of fate, he might well have been sitting quietly eating his lunch, his dog-collar proclaiming his profession while his face and body reflected the passing of many years of toil and effort he had had to endure.

*   *   *   *   *

When he got back from lunch the skies had opened the moment he climbed down from his horse with considerable effort. He groaned as his hips made contact with the unyielding ground. As he waited for his hips to readjust themselves he stood in the rain as it gained in volume the heavy drops splattering out from the wide brim of his hat and his face. He could see that Samuel Smith, the grocer, had placed a notice in his window that disturbed the tidy order of his mind. Being Sunday, the shop was closed but Thomas, always one to nip an issue in the bud, tapped on the door with his riding stick.

Eventually, after much huffing and puffing from the other side of the door, Samuel appeared showing his annoyance at being disturbed on his rest day, until he recognised the owner of the face.

"Bless my soul vicar. What are you doing out in this rain?"

Which, to Thomas, seemed like a fairly crass comment and that there had to be a seriously silly answer, but he could think of none; besides it was the man's only rest time in a long week. He walked in past a row of open-topped sacks each with a neatly written label proclaiming their contents. Samuel closed out the weather in the gathering gloom of the shop interior.

"Now Vicar, no doubt you have seen the notice and want to ask me about it?"

"Quite right, Samuel. This festival...this beer festival? Exactly what will this imply? I mean, is it just an excuse for the men of the village to drink themselves ever sillier, and on the Lord's Day I see?"

Samuel scratched his ample stomach, well rehearsed in his speech by his wife. "Well Vicar, you knows as well as anyone that the only day for relaxation is on a Sunday. Everyone works so hard six days a week just to earn a wage sufficient to feed the children."

Here, Samuel was crafty, knowing Thomas's love for all of the children in the village. "And, it's just a bit of fun really. We are going to have races; three-legged race, sack race, a sprint for the younger of us. Other things as well," he added seeing the vicar begin to look round his store, "like bat the rat and cowpat bingo...a bran tub and a coconut shy.

"Good, excellent, so why a beer festival?"

"Well, we need prizes don't we? William Hick down at the Black Bull is providing us with a cask of his ale and it will be half a gallon to each prize winner."

Thomas was still mystified and persisted in his enquiries. "But...festival? A beer festival?"

"Ah! Thought you might ask that one Vicar. Lads in Bickerton and Wighill are going to come over with some of their own beers they have brewed, like us and we shall have blindfolds on the men so we can find out which is the best ale. Then we all get to vote on it and the most number of votes will go to the winning village." He stopped for breath knowing he had been speaking too quickly as if he wanted to get it all over with. At the same time, a head appeared half way down the vertical ladder leading up to the bedroom.

"Hullo Agnes. A very good day to you," said Thomas beginning to think he had indeed called at an inopportune time.

"Ah Vicar, I thought you might be round. Your candles have arrived by the way. You may as well take them now." Agnes, as angular as her name implied and probably half her husband's weight adjusted her long skirt as she completed the climb down to the shop floor. She absent-mindedly ran a finger along the counter which gleamed of polish despite the gathering dusk. "Now't wrong with a bit of fun Vicar. And think of the children."

"It is the children I worry about Agnes, seeing their fathers get simple in the head. And what about James, James Fletcher, the swineherd? He never knows when to stop."

"True enough Vicar but Benjamin has said he will be attending...to see there is no stupidity."

Thomas was not at all sure the local constable would be able to control the youths from three villages at the same time but he had complained enough. He knew exactly when to speak and when to hold his tongue. "I'll take the candles Agnes and pay you tomorrow if I may. That way you will not be compromised into trading on a Sunday."

"Quite so Vicar," Samuel knew he had been neatly caught. "Your presence Vicar...at the festival. It will bring, well, quality to the show. It is always good to have gentry at things like this."

"We'll see," said Thomas turning to go. "By the way," he gestured to the rain still pouring down without the aid of a gutter on the shop roof. "You ought to buy some of those new steel ribbed umbrellas everyone is talking about. I'll buy one for a start."

"It might seem strange, Vicar, you walking about with such a thing in your hand as if you were lifting a stook on a pitchfork."

"You buy the umbrella, Samuel and I'll open the festival. How's that for a contract?" They all smiled. Honour had been satisfied.

"Good day to you both." Thomas pulled his collar high so his head almost disappeared from sight.

A vicarage of his own. Now that would be a thing.

Chapter Fifteen

'You Cannot Even See the Chancel Arch'

"Gentlemen! Ladies, we shall come to order if you please. Martha will you please take notes."

There was an abrupt silence in the room as Alfred Hiley called the meeting to order. Hiley was a man used to getting his way; besides he was worried as were all of the remaining people in the room. Mrs Martha Clough, the school mistress pulled a pile of quarto paper towards her and unscrewed the top from a bottle of ink. Thomas Fielden, here with his wife, adjusted a pair of fine pince-nez on his delicately chiselled nose and glanced around the table with long familiarity for such meetings.

Thomas Smith, the Parish Clerk was there, a dapper man in a well-pressed suit, his stiff collar cutting into his jaw line each time he gazed down on the agenda. Several others were in attendance, well-dressed folk who shuffled themselves into the most comfortable positions on their unyielding wooden chairs.

"We all know," he went on in a sonorous voice the better to match the mood of the gathering, "why we are here. St. Peter's is falling down. It is worn out...tired."

"Well," said the Clerk, "I'm not sure we can describe it like-" He was cut off in mid comment.

"Well, I am. I am the vicar so I should know better than all you put together in this room. St. Peter's has been ruined over centuries of use. Why, you can't even see the d-, begging your pardon, chancel arch, let alone the full height of the east window because of the under-drawing."

"But," persisted the Clerk, "that is not in itself a cause for rebuilding."

Alfred sighed as if to a young child not understanding something an elder had said. "Perhaps, Thomas, but the two windows in the nave are in a shocking state of repair and so is the roof. If we have to replace the roof then let us raise it a foot or two so we can see the arches again. And, we need a porch don't we? And a vestry is essential these days and, as for the ivy climbing all over the place, that's got to come off before the mortar is damaged further." He paused for breath. Privately, he was appalled at how badly his church had fallen into disrepair. Working and preaching day upon day until these fell into years he had not noticed how the fabric had deteriorated. Then one day, as if a veil were withdrawn from one's face the whole image of St. Peter's looked as if it had been drawn through a giant teasel from Leeds. Access to the tower roof had always been difficult and frankly, dangerous. The only way to check the tower roof was up a ladder that had to be two hundred years old. As he climbed stiffly to the first level from which he would go no further he could smell the pungent dampness of dry rot below the three bells. He was deeply worried they could fall.

He returned in mind to the meeting and allowed Martha to catch up with her note-taking all set down in a beautiful script, where she had filled the first page.

"If we lift the roof we will be able to see the entire east window...and get rid of that lath and plaster at the same time." It was Thomas Fielden, experienced in building who could see the possibilities.

"But, how much is all this going to cost? We shall need a faculty from York before we can do anything." There was more than one cautious voice at the table.

Albert waited until he had all of their attention. "I have some very good news on that front," he said, standing up a trifle higher as if to add to its importance. He waited again until he had caught the eye of Fielden who nodded his assent. "We've been back and forth over this so many times and never managed to raise the sort of funds we are going to require if we are going to carry out all of the works. So, I can confirm a most gracious and handsome gift from Mrs Thomas Fielden, also our two church wardens God bless them and I will match their offers should bring us very close to our needs."

The meeting broke down into a number of delighted discussions as neighbours began to understand that not only was their vicar putting his money where his mouth was but that the long wait to raise sufficient funding for the project was getting very close to succeeding.

Martha put down her long-handled pen and looked up at the enthusiastic crowd. "The estimates from the builder based on our plans and today's discussions have not changed this, raising the roofs, removing the ivy, building a new porch and a new vestry, moving the organ to its new home, new floor; it is going to come out at eleven hundred pounds. We need to add that the old squint currently sealed up will necessitate it being re-opened as the organist will be in a new position," she said speaking in a clear, precise voice as if addressing her pupils early in the morning. "With the flower festival, the Bring and Buy, the Strawberry Fair and our wonderful, generous benefactors we already have the enormous sum of one thousand pounds."

The vicar tried to dampen down the clapping and general hubbub but it was quite two minutes later by his gold hunter before calm descended once again. "There is one thing friends. St. Peter's will have to close. For the first time in five hundred years there will be no service." He wasn't sure if this was exactly true for he had once heard the Great Storm might have caused some services to be held elsewhere, but he felt the slight exaggeration would have been acceptable to those judging him on high.

"How long do you reckon, vicar, afore we can re-open that is?"

"Mr. Fawcett, our Architect from Cambridge believes it will be a full year. There is a lot of work to do and we don't know what we might find once the roof comes off."

Suddenly the idea of exposing their church to the weather seemed frightening, or at least began to raise considerable concerns. There had to be a very firm commitment from everyone. The sooner the work could be done the better.

"So, where do we go in the meantime vicar? We cannot worship in St. Peter's."

"Neither we can," replied Alfred. "But, I am sure we will all be invited to attend services in Thorp Arch...All Saints that is, not the Methodist place."

There was some laughter. "For the duration?" asked James, a market gardener whose devout wife would be full of questions on his return home.

"Sounds like a war," said Alfred. "It's not that bad...is it?"

Silence followed. It was not that there was anything wrong with Thorp Arch, indeed their church was far prettier than St. Peter's but the two villages had maintained a friendly rivalry throughout the centuries and they did have quite different views on a number of subjects. "Shame on you, we are all Christians here are we not?" There was a slight embarrassed air to the room. Silence continued. No-one wanted to poke their head above the ramparts or to be accused of non-Christian thoughts even though they were probably all agreed on the subject under matter.

"Tell you what. Think of our return next year. Practically a new church. Somewhere for the choir boys to change and somewhere for you to shelter as you arrive, shake your coats out so the floor does not get as wet. A lovely new parquet floor, smelling of pine wax, with Mrs Fletcher's good old elbow grease to give it that extra shine. And think of that nave soaring up close to God with a full view of the chancel arch and the east window. When you are bored with my sermon you will just have to lean your head back, the better to consider my words, while what you will really be doing is to examine our new roof."

They liked that one. "What a shame all of the old stained glass has gone."

"Yes, perhaps." Thomas did not like to be interrupted in full flow even if Martha was right. He knew modern Victorian glass could never match the exquisite *reds and blues* of the mediaeval times which one could see so well in York Minster.

Around him there was a stir, then a chatter of voices again. He was content as Chairman to let them discuss the ideas on their own. He sat back and lit his pipe.

"What about a new pulpit? Seeing as almost everything else is new," someone asked from behind his pipe's smokescreen.

"But, it is perfectly sound...and ancient. It goes back a long way in history. Think of the vicars who have preached from here."

"Exactly my point vicar. We don't want anything old in our church." There was a number of assenting voices. Victorian, they said, was right and good Victorian was Empire. If it was built in Victoria's reign then it had to be the best.

To Alfred though, this was a late and unexpected setback for his pulpit. It was seventeenth century with delicate design and one of the finest items to be catalogued in the terrier. But, for once, his forceful voice was muted. "You realise we have not even started but already we are adding to the cost. Who is going to pay for these extras if we cannot keep to what we have agreed?" It was a fair point "This is a work of art, the panels are pure gothic in design and age."

"And wood-wormed," countered the Clerk.

"Perhaps," interjected William Vincent, seeing the exasperated look on his vicar's face, "perhaps we could replace the panels leaving the rest of the pulpit which is in a satisfactory state. Tell you what Vicar. I will pay for its restoration and throw in a few other things as well."

To Alfred the whole point of the pulpit was the quality of the panels but he knew when he had to give way.

"That is very generous of you William. Thank you very much." There was little more Alfred could say on the subject. It was, after all, their church and they all felt very strongly about St. Peter's as it had sat on the top of their hill for as long as anyone could recall.

"I am going to request a faculty be granted straight away. We have waited so long to raise the funds and if we leave it any longer the ivy will be on the roof."

"Too late vicar," said Martha. "It is already well over the eaves."

"Then we had best get started even sooner. All those agreeing for us to go ahead, raise your hands."

There was no doubt in the minds of the gathering. The mood was unanimous for a 'Get on with it, for goodness sake' and the motion was passed. Services would just have to be shared at Thorp Arch until next year.

As the meeting was about to be wound up with discussions turning to any other business, Martha raised her hand.

"Vicar, perhaps when we re-open we could have some sort of special re-dedication ceremony. Invite someone of character, from York?"

"Capital idea, Martha, and we will get your children involved."

While Martha smiled back her thoughts were on the news she had just received that her school was to close the following year with all of her children being accommodated in the new school at Thorp Arch. It was a bitter blow to her pride for her reports had forever been of the highest standing, but the School Authorities were intent upon size and amalgamation, and she had no option but to agree. All she could now was to apply for any of the posts which might be offered in the future at the Industrial School along the road towards Thorp which also had an excellent reputation

*   *   *   *   *

William Fawcett, Architect and engineer, gazed down at the floor between his feet. He was a slim man, effete in some ways though his eyes betrayed the intelligence behind the lids. He sniffed as he examined the ground. Brailsford's men had lifted the cracked pavings throughout the length of the church. From the door to the tower to the window in the east, rubble and clay was strewn about untidily as it was removed in barrow loads. The men knew better than to leave the site in a mess at the end of the day but there was plenty of light with which to work. From the ground came a strong smell of dry rot and wood beetle dust and something more: the odour of ancient settlements. He was, however, more interested in the stone slabs undoubtedly marking the final resting place of six people, although the stones themselves were without any inscriptions. They thus had to be old, ancient even. There was nothing to indicate who or even what might lie below and whether there was anything there at all, but the Fairfax's jealously claimed rights to all of the graves if that is what they were seemed to be supported by this evidence.

Fawcett felt they had every right to ask that the ground be left untouched for they held documents showing that their ancestors had been buried in the floor many years ago. Certainly, he surmised, anyone buried below his feet had to be gentry, high-born gentry for that matter to have dominated the entire space available for burial within the church.

"Mr. Brailsford. A moment of your valuable time, if you please."

The builder stepped around a barrow of rubbish being loaded up for removal through the opening which had contained the south door. "I want the whole floor concreted; four inches will do on this compacted clay. When that is cured and not before, and not before all other work is complete," he looked up to the sky through the new tie beams now in position, "we will cover them with pitch pine blocks laid in hot pitch."

"Very well, Sir."

"And, another thing Mr. Brailsford. Fairfax, him yonder asleep in his decorated niche. I am not happy with the protection you have given him with just that single board. He's damaged enough as it is and the family will be upset if they receive further knocks from your men even if inadvertently."

"Very good Sir." He whistled through his fingers at two young lads shovelling clay. "Ere, you two, drop what you are doing and bring some boards in, that seven by two stuff in the back...and some rope. No fixings in the stone. Just secure 'is nibs from any damage. If you break off any pieces I'll break off similar parts from your bodies. Understand?"

"Yes guv." They understood only too clearly what was wanted. The boss's rope end was often in use causing rich words to fly within the church. The vicar had more than once remonstrated with Brailsford's men to ensure that that sort of language was kept for the Fox and Hounds in the evenings.

As the Architect turned away, satisfied, he gazed once more at the final resting place of a number of Walton's most celebrated residents. He had considered asking the Parochial Church Council for additional funds to pay for a brass plaque telling all who might have been interested just who lay beneath their feet but, with the contingency fund already running low he decided against it.

Two days later all that could be seen was a trowelled smooth, grey concrete floor of concrete. The Fairfax's were gone forever.

*   *   *   *   *

"Hymn number six hundred and two...Oh Jerusalem the blissful," intoned Alfred Hiley, resplendent in his full stole and chasuble. He looked across at his eminent guest, the Bishop-Suffragen of Beverley, Dr. Richard Crossthwaite, no less, a purposeful man intent on climbing the ladder of his chosen profession as high as he could manage. Attending and officiating at such functions especially after he learned the local press would be there was well worth accepting the invitation. As he recalled, the vicar had mentioned the local journalist would be attending at the time he had received the request. Besides, there would be a very good lunch afterwards and some well-chosen wines and port.

Alfred still found it difficult to recognise his own church. The roof angles were all wrong, well different, now much steeper than before with the nave ridge rising up and striking the Norman tower ten feet higher than before. The ivy had gone and the windows rebuilt. The new porch, he felt, merged rather well with the original stone so at last, Mrs Pawson could stop complaining about building a porch. But, best of all was the interior. Below his feet the pine blocks glowed with bees wax and the roof soared towards God as he had prophesized. He could see the chancel arch as clear as day including the pointed arch with the east window now clearly defined in its shape. In front of him the organ had been moved away from where it had half blocked penitents on their way to the altar rail and was reinstalled in its new alcove. Even better was the new door leading to the vestry.

Alfred felt good, inordinately good for he had got everything he had wanted...except for a single issue. The Bishop was climbing to his feet ready to mount the pulpit. The modern panelling crudely chiselled in his opinion lacked the love of the seventeenth century wood carvers and the new work looked somewhat out of place although his parishioners thought differently. It would need a cloth, a purple one maybe to hang down to cover some of the newness of the oak.

The Bishop's voice was alert, his address short, mindful no doubt of the lunch to come and the need for the congregation to return to work. There was a thatcher there particularly who wanted to get on with re-roofing cottages on the main street which had not been thatched for fifty years. Many a swallow dipping away from the flies on the cricket pitch had found a home within the thick straw from whence they would now have to find new nests.

His problem lay in the fact he simply could not help looking up towards the clean roofline; it made his Adam's apple shift forward each time as if it too was eager to gain a sight of the new trusses. He wondered if the Bishop was watching his antics then knew he was almost hidden from the view from the pulpit. The man's crisp voice was praising the congregation for their steadfastness during the long period when the money just did not arrive in the sort of quantities the Architect and the builder required.

Alfred's muse hovered, before falling back into time when this same church had been first consecrated five hundred and forty-one years earlier. So much water had flowed down the River Wharfe since then; the village had been visited by war, pestilence, poverty and feast, a great deal for one small church to manage. What enormous change the village had undergone while St. Peter's had remained like a rock in a raging storm, emerging after the wind and the rain to continue its services as it always had. Only the houses alongside its boundary wall and running down the street were ephemeral, always shifting never lasting very long. Just today he had been told that there was serious talk about pulling down another ancient cottage further down Main Street to make way for new houses. Some of its windows sagged at their heads as rot attacked the window lintels. The rabbit hutches which leant against the rear gable wall were grimy with filth. The rat population had exploded to the extent where they invaded back doors at will even in broad daylight.

"...God bless you all," said the Bishop crossing himself before bowing to his appreciative listeners and beginning to climb down the steps. He had finished in record time.

Surprised, his reverie broken, Alfred adjusted his collar. "Dear friends, do not forget tonight William Hanham is to preach here. I know many of you want to hear him, a special man indeed, so come early. We shall be taking an offering tonight also to help adjust the additional expenditure we incurred in these works." He opened his arms wide to encapsulate the entire building. As he spoke, one of the ancient bells began to ring out. It was the biggest, inscribed *'Michel Archangel'* and it began to send out a renewed message of hope. It vibrated the shop window and rattled a pile of neatly stacked tin cake cases; it upset a horse tethered outside making it stamp the ground with a shod hoof as it munched away in its nose bag. Further down the road the head butler at the Old Hall noted the chimes and signalled to one of his staff to inform cook that the party would soon be on its way for lunch.

At the Smithy, the red glow from the fire threw sparks towards the dusty ceiling. Gabriel lifted a hoof into his leather apron and pulled the old nails from the shoe in an easy motion of the pliers. Not for him the service of thanksgiving but he could hear the bell above the roar of the furnace as could several farmers out in their fields and it brought him a feeling of renewed comfort. The community needed its church.

On that day, contentment spread like a balm throughout the village, knowledge that everyone had contributed in some way or other to the success of the church restoration. What they could not have known, that in just twenty years the country would be plunged yet again into war, though this time the loss of life would be so staggering it would make that snowy ground in Towton appear like a road accident.

Chapter Sixteen

A New Use for the School

There is something inordinately satisfying in the sound of a fine willow bat being struck cleanly in its centre. The sound this time reverberated around the pitch and up the green hill to generate an echo as it ricocheted off the north wall of the church. It was followed almost immediately by several cries of 'Owzz- at' and polite clapping as the batsman walked towards the railway carriage which acted as the pavilion.

The purchase of the carriage had been a good deal done, five pounds exactly and it had been manhandled into position below the Fox and Hounds so it now produced not only two sets of changing rooms but a decent place for tea.

Walton Cricket Club, thought William Busby, vicar of St. Peter's, was one of those excellent institutions which best underlined all that was great in Great Britain. The 19/10d remaining from monies raised at the time of King George V's Coronation two years earlier had formed the financial basis for a Cricket Club and having as its first President, Edward Lane-Fox had been a real coup for the man was a fanatic about the sport and a skilled bowler who thus brought considerable strengths to the team. William himself had been inveigled into playing and was as a result fitter, leaner with a new found impetus for Saturdays.

It did mean he had to work in the evening on his sermon, often delayed by the proximity of the Fox and Hounds into whose cosy interior the team would troop after a match, captain leading, often triumphantly.

Taking on Bramham Park might have caused Lane-Fox some difficulties but he had already declared there were Chinese walls so no order of play, or tactics could be gleaned by the Bramham team who were to say the least, close to home.

That particular night, following another triumphal win and over a pint of ale, the team discussed the news that Scott had been beaten to the South Pole by a Norwegian fellow some months earlier! The other news, dismissed by some as irrelevant was a mess arising out of a little known town called Sarajevo. "It's too small, too far away and, anyway, what is it to do with us?" said the wicket keeper when the vicar tried to change the subject from the death of a British hero in the bitter wastes of the Antarctic.

"It's all to do with Alliances. The whole world is dividing itself up into sides. Germany's-"

"Germany is our friend. Victoria had German blood in her, and Albert was a German. No, they'll never go to war with us, stands to reason."

"What does that mean?" enquired William gently. "Where politics and power are concerned, that will count for nothing. And look at her naval power."

"Vicar, Vicar!" replied the wicket keeper, sweat shining his brow as he enjoyed his fourth pint. He had been instrumental in taking out five of the opposing teams batsmen and he felt justified in having a telling off by his wife on his return home later. "We've... we've got the best navy in the world. We'd thrash the hide off them."

On such words, mused William, are wars caused.

"At least it will not be fought in Great Britain. It won't be like Marston Moor just down the road when we were all personally affected. Let someone else take the pain for a change. Those frogs they need to be brought down a notch or two...the sods."

The landlord leaned over the counter. "Now then, Mr. Henry. I don't like that sort of language in my house if you don't mind. This is a respectable place."

"Yes, yes, I'm sorry George. I got carried away."

Well, just you mind your tongue in future." George completed his remonstration by wiping the top of the bar fiercely with a well-worn cloth as if to sweep the words as well as the spilt beer into the mild slops tray.

The noise increased in the same ratio as smoke from a dozen or more clay pipes as it filled the void above the standing men and added to the yellowing stain on the plaster between the wooden beams. With summer, the door out to Hall Park road was left open revealing three small boys sitting on the steps playing jacks with dried rabbit bones. Ordered to remain in place while their fathers enjoyed themselves, they had long ago stopped whining at the nightly ritual of helping dad carry home an open jar of ale. William tapped them on the head as he bid the team goodbye.

"See you in church tomorrow lads."

"Yes Vicar," came back three voices in unison though missing the bounce in their voices as, for example, when supper was announced on the table.

As he walked back up to the road his thoughts remained, not with the cricket match, enjoyable as it had been, but on the latest news from Europe. Henry, he was sure, had been wrong in saying he believed the war would never come because of the Palace's relations in Germany. And Victoria had complicated the issue as her family continued to marry, extending the links to most Royal houses on the continent.

He studied his next sermon's rough notes, feeling that a war, any war still seemed remote from the aspect of Walton. To reach the northern coast of France was a two-day journey from York, and what then? Britain did rule the waves and the Channel would therefore be protected, so the bloodshed, if it did come would not stain English soil this time?

He could not make up his mind about the likelihood of war though there a mood about the country which appeared to lead in one direction only. It was as though the British needed a good war every so often to ensure the world understood who ruled the waves. His notes lay in front of him: a rather trite passage on being a Good Samaritan to older folks. He tore the sheets in half and dumped them in the waste paper basket and took up his pen. He had a new subject for his people and one which, he hoped, would awaken them to the dangers ahead.

*   *   *   *   *

The whole month had been one of high temperatures and humidity causing the cricketers to miss catches as the ball slipped through sweaty palms. Downpours arrived as certainly as the milkman would call in the morning at the same time each day. John Whitehead gazed moodily out of a window onto the triangular village green which framed the front of his imposing house, as the rain poured from every gutter and cascaded down the front steps. He had closed the forge early as he always did on a Wednesday to give himself time to riddle the forge and clean up the yard of the piles of horse manure. Now the yellow slurry from the patient animals turned the path at the side of the house to a slimy porridge.

There seemed no end to the weather with matches being cancelled causing chaos to the game fixtures, compressing those left into a tight programme for the end of the season. The summer fête would be in jeopardy if it didn't start to settle down once again. August perhaps was always unpredictable and this year it acted as though it was rainy April all over again.

It was worse for the farmers. The barley was laying itself flat in great circular swathes as field after field succumbed to the weather. Let alone the loss of precious income, the Tad breweries would find themselves short if this continued and that would mean higher beer prices so Smithy repairs of non-

essential items would be put on hold. He shrugged his shoulders
aware there was nothing he could do to change the situation and
flicked his stub end spinning into the rain. There was a storm
coming he knew but one that was blowing hard from
Germany...and there were fourteen lads in the village all of
eligible age if they were to be called up in the future.

While he sheltered from the rain, a small but insistent
idea had crept into his mind. The school house, empty now
and forlorn after so much effort to find the funds and build
the school could come alive again. Walton needed somewhere
on a Saturday night where the young lads, and lassies could
meet under the approving eye of the organisers instead of
hanging around in Goosemoor Lane out of sight of their
elders. A band each Saturday, some cider and lemonade, boys
to the left chairs and girls opposite while any adults could
cluster round the two fires at either end. The dead jackdaws
would have to be removed from the chimneys first and
permission sought from Edward Lane-Fox but he was a
reasonable man who would be able to see the value of airing
the building to remove the dampness which had crept into its
soft stone.

A faint smile lit up the smudged and blackened face, as
black as any coal miner's. He acknowledged the four men
working in the road despite the rain, on the far side of the green.
Two, out of sight were in a long trench from where shovelfuls of
earth and stones appeared at a regular basis. The other two, well,
thought John, they were not doing much at all, though they were
both glued upon the growing pile of dirt. They had earlier
brought an enormous coil of cable on a wooden drum which was
being laid into the trench down Smiddy Hill as they went. In a
few days the black snake would run past the Smithy and he
could, if he so wanted, agree to sign up for the new 'lectricity
which was already the talk of Wetherby. With gas already
established in the village two years earlier some houses now
glowed at night with the strange green light from the mantles,

hissing like asps as if each was alive and talking to its neighbour.

All at once the workmen became lost in a washed out landscape as the storm descended. The men retired at last into a curved top tent where the water was thrown off away from where they had all crammed inside. It wasn't really large enough for four men in capes and the apprentice, a mousy, underfed lad in a cloth cap had to sit in the entrance with his cape over his knees as he defended his seniors from getting any wetter than they were.

That lad wouldn't last a week in any real war, John could see. His own children were well fed and dressed: his own boy would have a far better chance of surviving with flesh on his limbs and the absence of any rickets to slow him down.

There came a chatter and clatter of many feet. Materialising out of the gloom emerged a crocodile of children walking back from Thorp Arch after school. Each head was covered with a long scarf wrapped round down to their chests and held in place by a large safety-pin fastened earlier by their teacher. As they saw their homes come into view their faces lit up after the gloomy, dismal walk. Their sandwich tins were empty and so were their stomachs.

John peeled off two very wet children and shooed them round the corner to the Smithy where he hung their clothes up to dry near the forge. In vests and pants they ran across the yard to hug their mother.

"What's fer tea Ma?"

"Cottage pie with some mushrooms I picked, rice pudding and some of my strawberry jam," she replied studying the pinched cold faces whose hair lay flattened on their heads as if oil had been poured over them."But first, upstairs and put on a warm jersey both of you."

Considerable noise arose as a scramble began between the two children as they raced each other up the steep stairs past the best room where they were not allowed to go without special permission. Outside, a watery sun was trying to break through the still leaden sky. Everything dripped, forming puddles which lay in the deep pot-holes in the road.

As the four men packed away their tools and climbed onto their bikes to ride back to Wetherby the lights winked on in Walton House. As regular as clockwork, cocktails would be taken on the hour whatever the weather. The small party hoping to play tennis below the house had been driven indoors even as they arrived at the front door. Talk instead, had centred around Jessica's new tourer, much admired as it had been by William who had turned up at the same time to visit the cook who had been '...took ill with a bad back'.

*   *   *   *   *

In Westminster also, lights burned all night as the world slipped remorselessly into war.

Chapter Seventeen

'You Don't Understand, Sir'

The German P.O.W.s' in their drab, down at heel uniforms looked totally out of place as they filed out of the old School House to start a day in the fields. There was no denying their value, what with a million British soldiers remaining for ever under the mud of Passchendaele and Mons. Those left to farm the undamaged if overgrown fields found that jobs which should have been done automatically dependent upon the time of the year, like ditching and mucking out the byres were pushed further down the list or even just abandoned.

But, some bright spark in the War Office, appalled at the loss of life almost all at a very young age, suggested the P.O.W.s' be put to work to obtain at least some recompense for the disastrous loss of valuable labour. It might help the farmers, desperate to produce more food. The idea that the Germans might attempt to escape was dismissed, countered by the knowledge that these German troops knew their battalions remaining in France were starving on the Front, ensuring they would continue to work in the firm knowledge that here at least, they were safe.

The moustache bristling, exactly like his counterpart the English Sergeant-Major who guarded them, pulled his men into a semblance of a line. They all wore boots covered in cow manure and mud but looked well fed and fit. They jostled each other, laughing as their own *Oberfeldwebel* read out the orders of the day. He noted in his diary the date in November, that it was an abnormally cool and wet day just as so many had been in the past three months.

A car approached the gate and a Captain stepped out with a lightness of foot though he only had one arm. He wore the M.C. on his chest. Under his one good arm was a brown leather valise. His own Sergeant-Major snapped to attention.

"Good morning, sah. Going to be a wet one today, sah."

"I believe, Sergeant-Major you are going to be wrong there. Very wrong." The Captain's mouth twitched, though not unkindly, merely giving way to a small pleasure based upon some secret he held.

"Very well, sah, if you say so."

"I do Sergeant-Major. I do. Now, I see your prisoners are drawn up. Keep them drawn up if you please. How many of them speak English now?"

"Most of them Sir. All of them a bit here and there."

"Right. Let me through and call them to listen up." The wired gate swung open and the prisoners, seeing a British officer approaching snapped back to attention to show they were not quite beaten yet.

The Captain inclined his head. "Sergeant-Major, bring your men all of your men here as well."

"Yes sah." Mystified, his squad took up spaces behind him.

"Now listen up. Those of you, who do not understand me, ask your neighbour for I do not have a translator today." So saying, with one deft, much practised movement, he flipped the valise across the stump of his bad arm, flipped open the lid and withdrew a single sheet of typed paper. It was tinted in the standard yellow War Office communication pad.

"I am instructed by His Majesty's Government that at eleven o'clock this morning, November Eleventh One thousand and eighteen, all hostilities with Germany will cease." He kept them waiting for an instant in time, aware of the historical event unfolding. "Germany has surrendered and an armistice will be declared from this time."

Before he could continue there was an immediate and joyful outcry, not only from the small contingent of British troops but the Germans as well who clapped each other on the back. There was no need to translate the Captain's clipped words. After four years of unrelieved nightmare it was over and they could go home.

The Captain shook hands with the Sergeant-Major. "Remember, Sergeant-Major, they are still our prisoners, but treat them as fellow men."

"Oh yes, Sah. I will do that, Sah!" As he was speaking, first one woman, then another and another appeared from around the corner and stood by the gate on the corner of School Lane. It was as if they had been waiting, listening for good or bad news from the one-armed Captain. Another woman joined them clad in a one piece full-length black dress and hat. Her eyes were red raw, her mouth pulled down in despair. As she approached, the officer saw the group and walked over with a broad smile.

"The war is over Ladies. Germany has surrendered."

But instead of cries of joy, they shook their heads in dismay.

"Well, I thought you would all be delighted. Your men are coming home." The Captain felt not a trifle chagrined at the response to his news.

"You don't understand, Sir," said one of the women, clearly a farmer's wife with her ruddy face and calloused hands from picking potatoes. "Mrs Lister, here, she lives next door to the church but the Lord didn't help her in her hour of need."

"I'm sorry. She has lost a son?"

"Yes Sir, but it is the timing of it all that is so cruel; almost worse than losing your son. You see, Norman Lister was killed four days ago She has just heard. Your Generals must have been planning this for weeks. Why did they not pull the men back to save lives? Doesn't seem right, does it Sir?"

The Captain, shoes speckled with mud from the road, covered in manure, dropped his shoulders in dismay. "I'm so sorry, Mrs Lister. I really am."

A brief glimmer of a smile flickered across the woman's face though it never reached to her eyes. He seemed genuinely remorseful. After all, a lad of twenty-two or three maybe, who had lost an arm at the Front almost certainly, would have had no say in the decision to send her son to his death four days before the end of hostilities.

"Thank you Captain. That's very kind of you." She turned, followed by her village friends and walked back up to the Main Street, past the Post Office on her way home. Almost seven hundred years after poor Molly had died of the Plague at the Black Bull another death had come to the same building, a death borne not this time as a miasma on the night air but as a yellow telegram carried by a boy on a bicycle. It was known in the War Office in the bland parlance of the anonymous Ministry as a *B104-82* but to the receiver it was 'the dreaded telegram' where, even if a wife or a mother refused to acknowledge delivery by the boy in the blue suit, the inevitability of knowing he had died would be immediate and absolute. It did not need a boy on a bike or his telegram to tell the news of yet another loss.

"Perhaps," the Captain suggested to one of the women well into her eighties who had remained. Shawled, wrapped against the bitter weather, standing somewhat forlornly by the side of the gate where, almost certainly she had attended school in her youth, "perhaps the village could club together, hold a fête and find enough money to buy the church a fine clock in memory of the man. It would be seen from a long way off so the village would always be reminded of the sacrifice.

The old lady, whose rheumy eyes belied an intelligence burning under her head shawl, twitched her mouth as if to practice how to speak. There must, he calculated, be a thousand wrinkles on that face.

"I'll tell Mrs Lister, Elizabeth as is. You see, she already lost Alfred in seventeen. Norman was only twenty-one when he was kilt. He was a driver a good one, having driven a tractor before the war."

The Captain bowed, a curiously old-fashioned gesture before saluting and signalling to his driver. As the car swept away through the dung and the muck, reminding him of a Flanders field, the old lady, Bessie, looked back up School Lane following the car. To her left were great piles of clamps holding potatoes and turnips, safely protected with a thick lining of straw from the nip of the frost which always tried to blacken the crop before it was required by the troops. Her mind turned to the news.

Peace. The church would be full to bursting this Sunday so she had best get up early for William Busby always began his services right on the stroke of the hour. It was Monday, so there would be almost a full week of celebrations and coming to terms with the idea there was no need to work anymore towards winning this terrible war before the calm of the church.

But, there was a third man as well. Bessie had forgotten to mention to the Captain another man, with a strange name. Newton. Newton Williams. The village should, had to find the money for a clock, a big one so it could be read across the fields by the farmers...with gold hands and numbers, so it would sparkle in the sun. Walton needed a clock so the people could for ever know the time accurately. What with having to catch a train at Thorp Arch, or the bus for Wetherby or just to find out when the service started at St. Peter's.

There was the quick clop of a pony and trap and William Busby came round the corner too fast for an old lady. He saw the prisoners marching off towards Hill Field and realised he was too late to hear the news in person. He had turned round in the road and hurried back when the news swept like a gorse fire down Smiddy Hill.

"Is it true, Bessie? Is the war really over?"

"Oh, aye Vicar, so they says-"

"Thanks be to God. Now the lads can come home."

"'Cept them three lads of ours Vicar. Them's not coming home."

"Yes. They will be the subject of my sermon on Sunday. Sacrifice...no greater love...that sort of thing." He touched his hat and flicked the reins. The trap sprang forward its wheels forming two deep lines through the slurry.

The old woman sighed as only a woman, who had already lost her husband and a real friend, could do. Peace, perhaps, but at a terrible price.

*   *   *   *   *

The old school, now a community hall, or rather the grander title of Village Institute gleamed in colour under the balloons and flowers. The room had been polished and the earth closet cleaned and disinfected with a liberal dose of Jeyes fluid, the aroma from which still hung in the air behind the firmly closed back door. The volume of voices rose and settled down again as Colonel Lane-Fox Member of Parliament strode in on cue with his wife Mary. They both smiled warmly to Sir Guy and Lady Graham as they sat down in the front row. A boy detailed to do just this job, quickly and deftly removed the two reserved cards on the chairs beforehand. Parson Willie Thomas, in his first important event rose as Chairman for the evening. The hall was packed to capacity but Willie could be heard at the back of the room for everyone wanted to hear what was being said by the gentry of the village. It was not often they were able to rub, shoulders almost literally, with a Member of Parliament and there was considerable awe at his presence in the room.

Sir Guy studied the Programme printed especially for the occasion and noticed he was in fourth place after a recitation by his wife He was down to sing a song he had been practising for two weeks.

He had seen service in the last war to end all wars but he never talked about it, not even to his wife. He preferred to merge with the happy expectant throng whose faces gleamed from the heat of the coal fires in the December evening.

The Colonel was rising to his feet, introduced by the vicar who, without further accord, sat down and spread his feet wide in front of him so that he made a large lap with his cassock. Lane-Fox handed over an embossed, important looking document, quite official in its way, to Willie who had to stand up again as he received the gift of Walton Institute in perpetuity on behalf of the village. From now on, the Institute belonged to each and everyone who lived in the village, a place for dancing, Christening parties, Parish meetings and the occasional auction. At least that meant the pub could get on with the business it did best, selling beer rather than cater for Tomlinson's auction and sales as had always been done in the past.

There was a huge cheer from the villagers packed in behind the dignitaries followed by *'for he's a jolly good fellow'* to which the Member of Parliament blushed and kept a tight hold of his wife's hand. He was used to making speeches in the House, opening fêtes but direct praise was something that Eton and Oxford rather frowned down upon considering it inappropriate to be singled out for any individual achievement. Instead, Lane-Fox waved his hand above the crowd for a moment or two to acknowledge the cheering. The India office beckoned and with it came a new sense of responsibility. These good people had wanted somewhere to meet for as long as anyone could remember; a simple need as simple as their lives. The school house would never be a school again and it was of little if no use to anyone except perhaps as a store or a barn. Let them have their Hall and they would give him their vote. It was a simple swop.

He felt change in the air and he was part of that change. Having sold off some of his old thatched cottages to make way for spacious new Council houses, the village was demanding better accommodation with every month that passed.

"Internal toilets for goodness sake!" he had exclaimed to his wife after receiving a report from his Estate Manager "Whatever next? A bath with running water I suppose."

What he found most difficult to keep abreast of, what with his duties in London every week, was the blurring and merging of the seasons. Once, the four seasons had ruled his life as immutably as St. Peters church sat on Walton hill. By seeing the food on his plate, his cook at the back door with a gardener or two with their baskets laden with vegetables and fruits, the ploughing championships, the Harvest Festival: there were so many of them he could almost fill a calendar every day of the year. Today, Fordson tractors sliced up the ground earlier and faster. Everything, he observed, was sooner so a piece of autumn was bolted onto the back of summer and spring was pushed back towards winter as far as it was possible.

Of course, when the weather decided to be 'difficult' as when a winter would endure until April, just as summer rain storms could beat down the barley then he knew they had taken the risk too far and they had to retrench for a while, but the writing was on the wall for all land owners. It was a time for change for everyone; the war had altered the social order beyond recognition and there was to be no going back to the old social way of life with the touching of forelocks and the paying of tithes.

It was time to lift his hold on Walton. Bit by bit, he would not do it all at once, but he could see a time in the future when every house would be owned by a freeholder. It was time to go.

Chapter Eighteen

This Man Moseley

"Don't talk so daft man. You'll never get there." It was Ada to her husband Joseph, determined and slightly knowledgeable: in other words at her most annoying. He was always a mad buggar, she thought and yet here he was again saying he will walk into Boston Spa in these conditions...it was just plain...daft.

The dilemma had arisen because they had both climbed onto the bus headed for Boston Spa, a single Decker without a number, along with a dozen others. The bus stop at the top of Smiddy Hill had icicles hanging six inches long from the sign. For as far as they could see the landscape was white: but not just white, for Ada could see massive drifts up against the hedges which had shielded Wetherby Road from the south-westerly's to some degree. Above, beech trees groaned as their over-loaded branches squealed over each other. The snow plough arriving up the hill at that moment pulled by two sweating dray horses struggled to make any impression.

"Will you get to Boston?" she asked the conductor.

"Maybe, maybe not. It's the hill up from the bridge I'm not sure about. No-one has been able to tell me anything about conditions over there."

Harold Huby, the driver was swaddled in a donkey jacket over his uniform, strictly against the rules though no-one in the depot was going to argue with him today. Shut up in his cubicle at the front he was unable to communicate to his conductor except by a series of well-practised hand signals. A new one had just been created whereby the man's fingers were held horizontally before being drawn across the throat.

"All aboard! Hold tightee!" The bell tingled in the cab and the bus started forward down Wetherby Road. It managed to get round the corner at which point Ada considered all things being equal that they might make it. The conductor had just plucked two tickets from his hand-held rack when, with a considerable scraping from somewhere below the bus it rose up on compacted ice. Black smoke issued from its exhaust, gears grated in double-declutch and most if not all passengers willed the vehicle forward.

It was to no avail. "We ain't goin' nowhere," declared Joseph, in double-negative form, a groom at Walton Cottage. "I'm getting out." At which Joseph, a sprightly sixty-two year old stomped down between the rows of shopping bags perched atop thick wool coats, and climbed down.

In the distance, five men were approaching on foot from the direction of the railway station. One of them was Arthur Westcott the vicar who had spent ten years travelling from Thorp Arch to Walton every day.

"You can't go on. The Causeway's blocked and even if you did get past, the bridge is impassable." The vicar's eyes were streaming with the bitter cold. His nose looked as sore as a whitlow on the end of a finger and Ada could see the vicar made sure his handkerchief touched his fleshy nose only lightly. Nonetheless, as society required, everyone raised their hats to everyone else before replacing them quickly to prevent the snow providing its own mantle.

"The snow plough and a couple of extra drays will get the bus out of this but it is going nowhere for the time being and certainly not today. Nor will there be any other buses until we are assured we can get through. We had best all walk home."

The passengers turned in unison able, thankfully, to put their backs against the flurries of snow. Arthur took up with the complaining Joseph.

"I shouldn't worry about a bit of snow Joseph. This will pass in due course but the news from London isn't going to go away in a hurry. This man Moseley, he's stirring up hate with these Fascists of his."

"Even he seems irr...irrele..."

"Irrelevant?" offered the vicar helpfully.

Joseph grunted an acknowledgement. "You knows what I mean Vicar. But people are starving in Wetherby. There is no work anywhere save on the farms and there is no money in that for a married fellow." Joseph spoke with considerable feeling. The Depression, like a dead shroud over the whole country was destroying families as it settled its dead hands in every town and village. Men were leaving, desperate to find work, any work. Even the shop had brought in piles of cheap canned food and kept the prices as low as they dared. Arthur knew it had helped.

The news, transferred through the grille of the Post Office on the counter was of Hitler and Moseley as his poodle offering work if only the people voted for them. It was tempting to cross over despite knowing the hate and viciousness which accompanied the demands.

As Smiddy Hill came into sight, Arthur knew he had more important things to do than worry about silly salutes and jackboots. There was Constance at the Lodge with a difficult birth just behind her needing comfort and reassurance that her husband would find work in Sheffield and would soon come back to see the new baby.

*   *   *   *   *

At his sermon the following Sunday, Arthur walked up the wooden steps to the pulpit as he had done countless times before. He let his congregation – not a bad turnout he mused – hang in suspense before he went to pick up his notes. He took in the pinched faces of the labourers; even Hiram the tailor looked as though he could do with a decent meal. Only the farmers and servants in the two big houses showed a plumpness of face or figure.

When he began to speak he allowed his voice to drop, dropping his loud, educated syllables from the room. This brought the attention of the parishioners as quickly as any exhortation; quick glances were exchanged and telegraphed from pew to pew. The shuffling of feet stilled and Isaac's powerful bay mare, 'Bonny' could be heard stomping her feet impatiently outside on the iron-clad ground.

"Today," began the vicar, staring down now without his notes,"today I'm not going to preach to you. Instead, you will all be able to go home and prepare for your lunch, or clear some snow, chop wood, feed your pigs. But before you do and because the great Depression is all around us and within us you must, every each one of you consider who might sit with you this Sunday lunch. Can you clear the snow for someone less able to do so themselves? Do you have some chopped wood, or better still some logs for a neighbour who may not have any? Go out and feed someone else's pig who might not have enough scraps for themselves let alone their animals. Everyone has a pig along the Main Street but not everyone has the food to feed it and dumb animals need care and love just as much as us." This was a fairly controversial comment to make but he rolled on without stopping. "This village has always helped its own. It always will, so when you are stuck in a snow-drift in a bus, just remember you have the money to buy a ticket and cash in your pocket to go and buy in the shops of Boston and Wetherby."

Joseph looked up at his vicar and inclined his head forward, acknowledging the thrust of his words.

"And a secular note to end with. Anthrax has again affected sheep in the area. Be especially vigilant if you are at Wetherby market. I know a lot of you men like to go there especially if you have nothing else to do. Some of you might remember the outbreaks here in the Eighties and the Nineties bad times. We don't want to encourage it back."

Several farmers pursed their lips as he spoke. Somehow the vicar was always on top of the news likely to cause distress to one or more families. As he was shaking hands with his parishioners' one farmer from Laurel Farm spoke up. "They need to clean up that there market vicar, afore the disease gets to the cows."

"Remember James, it can spread to you through the skin so don't have any cuts showing." James smiled ruefully as he held up his ungloved calloused hands. They were covered in small cuts and scratches and a savage burn on one of his wrists. "Right vicar, I'll take note of that advice." As they all trooped down the slippery path where three phaetons waited with their ponies draped in heavy rugs, Albert knew that this cold, applied to people without enough warm food and fuel, would kill them as surely as the Anthrax.

Chapter Nineteen

Could Have Blown Us All Sky High

"Godamnit!" The expletive spilled from his mouth as old man Percy held out a piece of paper "Begging your pardon Vicar, of course, but, where is it all going to end? We've lost our rights to walk down to Thorp Arch across the fields what with this here Munitions Factory and that's now attracting the bombers, we can't ring our bells unless we are invaded and now we are going to lose all of our railings."

Parson Thomas as he was known to everyone took the letter rather ungraciously knowing of the order and unable to make further comment. It was, after all, an order issued by Parliament and he was not about to set up a one man action group. The Government's Emergency Powers Act allowed them to apply themselves to anything they saw fit to be involved in and one of those was to take away all of the railings and spare metal in the country. The issue to Percy was that there was so little notice.

Percy continued to grouse. "It is the sixth today and they are coming on the fifteenth. That is just over a week from now."

"But what does it matter to you, or anyone else for that matter. Whether it is a week or a month, it will happen and, meanwhile, the iron is going to go to build more tanks and guns. As for the bombs, the munitions plant here and at Champagne Whinn bring welcome work."

"But not welcome bombs-"

"One man slightly injured, not badly thank the Lord and that was at Marguerite Hepton's hospital. And the railway they have built. After the war maybe we can benefit from trains coming right up to our door?"

The old man sneezed hard into a spotless handkerchief. He knew the vicar was right in what he was saying, he only wished he might be more sympathetic in his listening. The trouble with the vicar was that he really did not want to listen to the griping of the village. He wasn't good at holding hands and saying things will get better if they clearly were not going to do.

And, there was full employment in the village especially for the women. The farms were all ploughing up their meadows; at least they would be as soon as the winter released its grip on the ground. With fuel so scarce the farms had turned back the clock reintroducing horses but even they could not start the ploughs until the land softened.

Parson Thomas returned the letter with a peremptory flick of his hand as though he wanted to ensure he was not carrying any of the responsibility for the order. Gates, posts and chains as well as garden fences were going unless the owner could show they were required to hold back animals within the fields which were then excused by the Clerk to the Council. His beady eye missed nothing in his search to meet his quota of iron and steel. Aluminium pots and pans had long gone for Spitfires and Hurricanes, taken away in a truck which had trundled down Main Street slowly so villagers could rush out to show their support by throwing anything that came to hand. They thus threw in far too many pans. There were a number of wives the following year who had to borrow large pans to make piccalilli in the winter and Rhubarb jam in the spring.

The news from all Fronts was absolutely dreadful so a keen eye was needed to read behind the lines of 'historic stand' and 'our troops fell back in an orderly fashion,' to know that England was losing the war. Rangoon and Singapore had both fallen and the British Army had withdrawn from Crete but it was in the Atlantic, an area often forgotten to land-locked villagers that caused the greatest worries resulting in the shop's shelves exposing themselves to daylight for the first time in years as the tinned food, once packed in rows ran down or petered out.

Percy had been quite right in saying that nothing was sacred these days but no-one wanted to hear the church bells ring out unless it was confirmed they were a celebration of the end of the war. The following week the villagers walked up and down the Main Street understanding properly for the first time that a considerable part of the road now appeared almost bare without its screens of rails. Men had arrived in a truck, certain of their position and in what they were doing, and brought with them powerful saws which bit into the rails along the top of the stone bases. It was all over in no time and the team moved up the street to a new position. By four o'clock that afternoon the truck was piled as high as it was possible, dogs sniffed the opened up walls and tea was served as usual as night fell.

The forge, in its prominent position showed only five feet of bare stone paving between the pavement and the house. It was as if someone had stolen the private part of each house, opening it up to embarrassment in its nudity, and certainly, a loss of privacy. It soon passed of course as the next wave of bad news engulfed the newspapers but it was realised that the rails would never come back and a part of most Englishmen's homes was gone forever.

The munitions plant, when it was announced that it was going to be built half a mile from the village, caused considerable alarm. '...it was just over the hill;' '...just there; '...able to remove Walton with one match if something went wrong, a simple miscalculation or just plain forgetfulness.'

To the west, down Goosemoor Lane it was almost as bad though no-one knew if ten thousand detonators would cause as much damage as a stack of high-explosive bombs or shells. This site was, however, much closer to the church, the parson could see, measuring distances in long strides of his booted feet and the knowledge he had walked the lane on many an occasion. Perhaps the hill would help? The risks were high, the village knew that only too well, but times were dangerous anyway and if the Germans invaded Britain the whole exercise would be inconsequential anyway. More information came to light as the women began to take up work within the fenced off area and news began to filter back despite the Official Secrets Act.

On arrival for their shift each employee had to line up in turn for a thorough search of their clothing. Anything at all which was likely to cause a spark or a flame had to be removed. Thus, cigarettes and matches, metal hair combs, even snuff boxes had to be left at the Contraband Office before entering the factory area.

Elthspeth was one such from Hall Park Road as she glanced down the grid of new roads like an American city and took in the massive earth bunds each covered in grass sods which encircled the operational areas. There was a determined grittiness about the whole place bringing the war right up to their front door, which had been until then far removed to Leeds and beyond. Having given up her shoes and removed her cigarettes and matches Elizabeth queued up to put on her one-piece uniform something like Churchill's siren suit and all in the same colour. All at once they began to look like clones of some gigantic Orwellian machine. The clothing was, of course, designed so it would not snag on any piece of machinery. Her own outer clothes and hand bag were put in an over-sized black linen sack and hung on a hook as if she was back in the gym of her school. Just as she was wondering how she would tell the bosses from the workers it was explained to her that everyone wore a coloured turban. Elthspeth would wear a red one; the next tier up the line was blue – those were the 'onlookers' the checkers, and the supervisors, the really important people who made decisions wore yellow.

What really did annoy the army of women to begin with was the instruction to wash their faces before applying a special face cream. They were assured it was the best quality cream and it was there to prevent their skin absorbing explosive powders. In hind sight they realised it was for their own safety and it did smell quite nice. She found the aspect of making up with a whole line of other ladies off-putting on her first day but Rose, in front of her said that at least they had their own beauty parlour to make up in, out of view of the men. Once this was done the last thing she had had to do was to put on uncontaminated rubber shoes.

Parson Thomas was reassured when told the women did practise before they started on the real thing with dummy explosives until they were adept at handling the dangerous materials.

Despite all of these precautions there came a day when William was sat as usual at his grinding machine where his job was to grind down aluminium blocks arriving daily on the trains, into fine powder. As Bill completed a pot of powder he would lift it out of its position under the grinder and prepare it for transport to the next department. On this occasion he saw something poking out of the powder which had settled down to a level position. Sifting with his fingers he found, to his considerable alarm a match and, on further inspection a further eight appeared.

"Oh my God, Ethel! Ethel! *Ethel!*" he repeated. "Come here please. At once!"

Ethel, in a yellow turban walked over quickly as she heard the note of alarm in his voice. He was a quiet man by nature and for him to be raising his voice above the 'Workers Playtime' radio was enough to galvanise her into action.

"Yes Bill? What is it?"

Carefully, the operator withdrew all nine of the matches from his hand, one by one. He had decided to stop breathing. "They were in the pot, sort of hidden. What shall I do with them Ethel?"

"Take them out through the emergency door Bill, and wait on the path. I will have you met there and they will take them off you. Do you understand?"

"Why me Ethel?"

"Because there is no-one else Bill. Besides, there might be a spark in exchanging them to someone else." As she spoke she snatched up a black telephone. "Hut Seven here. Ignitable material found here. Yes, rear door. Bill Farrington will meet you there. He is holding nine matches."

Slowly the operator walked to the emergency door which was opened for him. He held the matches out in his sweating hand as if it was diseased. His face was wrinkled up in dismay as the girls stared at him in horror.. He glanced back as he went through the door but Ethel was already back on the telephone, this time to the Special Detective Force.

Gradually calm returned along with the pale-faced grinder, who was now holding nothing more dangerous than a cup of tea.

That night in the Fox and Hounds the news had leaked out and a journalist from Leeds was dispensing pints to anyone who could offer information not of a secret nature. Some felt he should not be asking any questions at all. "Don't give Gerry the opportunity for a laugh," said one. "Could have blown us all sky high."

"Yes, but what were they doing there in the first place?" said his drinking friend. Neither of them worked at the plant, both being cowmen thus exempt from service, but it did not stop the alarm. Wild stories of Walton disappearing in one giant hole if one small match had been struck did not help the mood.

The journalist was there because there was a story to be told. German spies perhaps smuggling in the means to set the place alight; a single villager, not necessarily from the village itself for employees came in by train from as far away as Leeds, or was it simply an employee desperate for a cigarette at break times who had smuggled the matches in one by one?

It was a detective mystery to rival Agatha Christie which would baffle the Special Detective Force for months and caused the Contraband Section to redouble its efforts in their checks.

As time went by and no arrests were forthcoming the villagers forgot their worries as other more frightening events began to supersede their local issues.

Through all this, life had to go on because there was no option. Churchill had decided to fight to the end, or at least in the hills and on the beaches. There were ration books to deal with and to be kept alongside the purse for without it money was useless. Orange juice, in small brown bottles for young children became available though it did not taste anything like orange juice should. Better, came Radio Malt served on a table spoon with the sticky end wrapped quickly and expertly in a tight loop before it was allowed to drop onto a clean shirt for school. Father coming home on leave found trains packed with troops, the ice-cold carriages jerked constantly as they stopped for no apparent reason. Vegetable plots blossomed again for the second time that century, home-reared chickens and rabbits added variety to the otherwise deadly dull food and Walton hung suspended in time, neither moving forward to new ventures nor dropping back

And, through it all, Willie Thomas conducted his sermons to an ageing congregation. There were few young men for they had all been called up to war. The young women were in and out of church, only some being what he liked to think of as regulars. Alternating shifts played havoc with attendance and any comments of "...sorry but I'm up at the *ROF* tomorrow" had to be met with "...of course, I'll find someone else for the choir. I quite understand."

But, he didn't really understand, did he? It somehow felt to him it was all wrong, this idea of women playing at soldiers and at war itself. Perhaps land girls had a place although often they could not lift the heavy machinery even if they did fill valuable gaps in the farmers' calendar.

But, he mused, to fill shells with explosive, intent as they became on exceeding their quotas to bring pride of place in a particular hut's output, to kill other human beings albeit

Germans: "Well!" he exclaimed on many an occasion, "it just doesn't seem right."

To most others though, they felt it was exactly right to be doing a job so that the menfolk could be away at the Front. Without the women to take the place of otherwise sorely needed troops and sailors the country did not have a chance. With them, Britain standing alone might somehow find an edge, a lever under which they might shift the German boot back across the Rhine.

Chapter Twenty

Man About Town

He was a bachelor, everyone knew that. In fact, it was the first thing his congregation learned about the debonair, beautifully suited man-about-town vicar.

He had arrived in his car and accepted, gratefully, a rather liberal whisky and water from the church wardens who had taken the trouble to find out his favourite tipple. A small group had been rounded up to meet their new vicar. The drink was the more welcome when one knew just how difficult it was to find good whisky these days, let alone a single malt. It had slipped down his throat in the rotund face, as his thinning hair clung precariously to the sides of his head as he creased into a smile.

"Heaven be," he added to the assembly, most of whom were drinking elderflower cordial without a lot of cordial as there was a current shortage of sugar.

"And, is it your intention always to remain a bachelor vicar. Or just not yet found the right person?" This came from a behatted, ample bosomed lady from just outside the village.

Lionel Griffith had fenced off this question on so many times before he was quite skilled in his reply. "Ah, my good lady." She wasn't a lady as such but he did not yet know her name and besides, he could see she would rather like the title bestowed upon her. "Without the distractions of children I can spend more time on my Ministry."

"But...a wife can be so...helpful. There are all of those fêtes, those little events for fund raising which are so important in a small village like Walton."

"I intend, dear lady," he boomed in a voice which, they knew, would be heard in every corner of their church. "I intend to take a house-keeper who will be all things to me: secretarial, cook, cleaner, and organiser."

One or two of the women present wondered quite what he intended by the remark. His whole presence in the room, the way his eyes settled upon the younger ladies eyes made him a 'ladies man' who could well stir up trouble even unintentionally in the village with some of the more traditional attitudes and values of the menfolk.

One of the prettier ladies estimated quickly he would be six feet at least in his stockings, and there was no doubt he was good looking into the bargain. With his obvious if under-stated wealth, through the family no doubt, he was a 'catch' for anyone.

"Well Vicar. Apart from your church duties you are enrolled on the cricket club committee, AGMs' are compulsory I'm afraid as well as the Parish Council of course."

"It needs a lot of care and attention these days," Lionel replied thoughtfully, "We may have landed in Sicily but the war is far from won. Next, the Government will want us to plant vegetables between the graves, where ever there is space I suppose." Lionel looked round for another drink and seeing none in the immediate offing began to wave his empty glass casually in the air as he talked.

The parishioners who encircled him were not sure whether they should laugh at the small joke or take him seriously not knowing what his views were on the war, and nothing on his politics. For all they knew he might have very fixed ideas about keeping to the exact word of every Government decree of which they arrived like snowflakes these days. Or, maybe he had no wish to be involved in the minutiae of village life. Some if not many of these regulations with which they all had to live were quite silly, with some showing a greater degree of stupidity than others.

John, another church warden was trying to trace his accent but it was smothered by his school and university. He should have been an actor in another life, he felt. The man projected himself as if he was on a stage with the village as his audience. "Hmm," he contained his thoughts inside. The man would have to prove himself first to these hard-working people.

And it did not take long to demonstrate that their vicar was not one to be seen about the streets shaking hands on the way. He was more often observed behind the wheel of his car. He would wave happily enough but drive on past with a face intent of going somewhere even if no-one knew where. Neither did he take any interest in cricket although he was a compulsory member. But when the day the church bells had rung, not for invasion but for victory he had been there to celebrate. The plain facts were he did not understand the game nor its rules and preferred the magnificent sport of Kings. Gradually it dawned on the village that when he was often to be seen driving away from the village it was towards one of the newly re-established race courses which encircled his home. There was nothing wrong in that they knew and he proved kind enough when someone was in trouble but there was just something missing, a lack of warmth, 'no bedside manner' said one, though this was still dangerous talk about such a man of the cloth.

His voice echoed around the church filled to bursting as everyone wanted to join in the feelings of goodness and just of being alive.

He ended his sermon on a secular note. "We must work to get street lighting into Walton. It is not right that young girls should have to walk in the darkness, lit only by a small torch, in these days of...of...greater emancipation. The war has changed everything, and forever. Women, ladies will be seen as being equal in every way to men in the future and they should not feel afraid of walking in the gloom and the dark of our streets."

Not all of the men believed their lady-folk would ever be on the same standing as themselves, even if privately they knew and acknowledged what they had achieved on the farms in the war and in the home. There were several 'hear-hears' in the congregation.

As the nation struggled with rationing worse than it had been in the war, with shortages of everything, it felt to many as if the war was continuing or even getting worse despite the removal of the war dead lists from the newspapers. In the midst of this gloom came a winter to match all winters in living memory for the amount of snow dropped on the village roofs and streets. It became a real effort to continue to clear the drifts as it began to pack up on the sides of the streets. The two-horse snow ploughs commissioned to the Simpson farm kept the main paths clear but there was no school for it was nigh on impassable to walk down to Thorp Arch. Instead, children played endless games of snow balls when they were not helping in the kitchen with their mothers cooking up never-ending bowls of soup.

The gloom and doom within the village was heightened by this lack of lighting in the road and had become a bit of a sore point in the Parish meetings but it had been felt during the war they could not ask for lamp standards made of steel when the material was making tanks and guns. But peace had come and there was now no need to hold back for the greater good of the nation. He needed to develop a pressure group with some influence on the local or even national newspapers or with the M.P. to get what most people in England felt was commonplace.

Lionel did not suffer as much as many others had with the shortages which had arrived since the end of the war. Being a bachelor he was almost invariably asked out to Sunday lunch as they queued, as they had done for centuries, outside the church following another powerful sermon. There was no doubt he enjoyed the pleasures of life and recounted many tales of racing before the war, tips for horses which were inevitably provided with a caveat in case one of his parishioners placed a bet on his advice. He would talk of other parts of England where he rubbed shoulders with the landed gentry, he not being one of them himself though he could hold his own in any society.

Throughout all this, there came a gradual but insistent mood of the erosion of his place in the hierarchy, a feeling of better days as Britain moved out of that cold winter of shortages. The vicar had always been a man to whom you looked up to and respected and, in earlier days, touched your forelock to as you passed by. He was classed alongside the doctor and the bank manager, a man who was better read, more able to deal with the greater issues in life as well as local crises and surely the right person to marry your daughter or, eventually to bury you in the manner in which you had laid down in your Will. He was in fact, upper middle class.

Life was controlled, certain rituals had to be observed and there were few challenges to his edicts, his decrees or just his plans for a new style to next year's fête.

Lionel woke up that morning realising life had changed forever: he was just unsure if it was for a better or for a worse life. The trigger, which had set him on a mental journey, was an early Sunday morning as he pulled up at the church in his car from Thorp Arch to take the service. There was, he reckoned, not a bad congregation walking in twos' and threes' up Main Street and past the shop. It was of course closed being Sunday in general and for shopping in particular, shuttered windows declaring its allegiance to the complex rules of trading in those days. It then struck Lionel that of the fifteen or so ladies of all ages slowing down as they came up the steps that only those well into their seventies or older were wearing a hat. Had he just not noticed in his services or was this a one day phenomenon where many women had decided a hat was not for them today;

that this fashion omission would disappear as soon as the next Sunday came round?

The teenagers were the worst, but, he opined they always had been. Surely a head scarf if nothing better or a coloured ribbon tucked into plaits would be an indication that today was special and for that one should make a special effort to look good? One of the delights of his sermons had been to gaze down from his pulpit onto a flurry of feathers and coloured corduroy which would tilt back from time to time as one or more of the local women strove to see if their vicar was focussing his mind on them.

There was no doubt about the man, several ladies would chatter, no doubt in their minds, he was a good-looking man with a generous purse when it came to handing out monetary support for the Strawberry Fayre or buying a spare pie at the Harvest Supper raffle. But...no hat at all?

He got out of his car in an immaculate grey suit and threw an all-embracing "Morning Gentlemen, Morning Ladies" as he swiftly made his way up the path to duck low as he passed under the chancel door. It had never been high but to a six foot man bending down from the waist was essential if he was not to knock his forehead on the stone ogee arch. He stopped for the moment in front of the altar winded after the rapid escape from his parishioners and tapped his chest where his heart was to indicate to himself he had a touch of angina. It had happened on a number of other occasions though he dismissed the thought as soon as it arrived in his mind.

Inside the vestry he said good morning to his organist.

"John, have you noticed anything different about women lately?"

"No, Vicar can't say I have. What exactly do you mean?"

"Ladies are not wearing hats anymore. Well, a considerable number that is."

"No Vicar can't say I have." The man was becoming metronomic in his replies. "But, these days, anything goes, doesn't it?"

"Does it John? Does it? And men, they seem to have given up as well. Nothing to take off when they enter the church. It was always a sort of ceremony wasn't it? Makes them a bit...naked so to speak, without a hat," he ended lamely.

The organist shuffled his music sheets together urgently trying to communicate his need to get to his stool. It did appear as if the vicar was off on one of his witch-hunts again which would reach every part of the village within the week.

"Sets us apart from those Catholics though, doesn't it? They always cover up even their shoulders. I've seen them on my way here sometimes," he supplied a reasoned response he believed. "Now Vicar, if you could just..."

Lionel wasn't sure if this was an optimistic or a pessimistic point. "Next thing John, they'll be coming to church without a tie."

"That's a bridge too far Vicar, I'm sure."

"Maybe John, but I feel it in my water. It's coming, a sort of devil may care attitude to almost everything we do and know."

During his sermon on the pace of life against the solidity of the church he was on several occasions distracted from his notes by his need to count bared heads. He came to the conclusion that over fifty percent of those gathered in his church were bare.

It was not going to be a good day for the vicar of Walton. As the couples streamed out of the south door he noticed something new and wondered if he was becoming paranoid on the subject of worship. No slight bow at the waist; no eye to eye contact as someone would seek out solace or strength through a handshake. The church wardens were everywhere as usual, collecting up hymn books and placing them in neat stacks of five but one would expect them to be... slightly deferential perhaps, he pondered. On second thoughts the phrase jarred in his mind as it should so he replaced it with a modified 'respectful' instead.

Yes, there was no real respect in the queue. Warmth still emanated from the married ladies though these days they fenced with him as much as he to them. The men looked at their watches for it was four minutes past the hour and the Fox and Hounds would be open for a pint of mild or bitter. The man didn't play cricket and it was often told that he placed considerable sums of money on the horses just at a time when they were working the day out in Leeds or ploughing nearby in the fields.

Lionel was losing touch because the war had opened his people's eyes to the 'gentry.' They had marched and drilled alongside these landed and titled folk finding them as ordinary, or 'normal' as they fought and died in the same trenches and the deserts of north Africa. The war had been a great leveller so that for the first time in history men no longer felt they had to doff their hats while their wives curtsied at the approach of a dog collar. And Lionel felt this loss of power, of his command and his place in society. No longer would the ladies nudge each other as he approached them where they stood behind a stall selling home-made cakes. Sure, the greeting would be open and welcoming but, too quickly, their eyes would roam away to seek out another view of a local cricketer with his shirt unbuttoned to expose a comely chest.

He was still distracted that afternoon when he had to minister to a Christening of a local baby boy. The duty church warden had been busy in the vestry when the family arrived with attendant god parents, who he had already spoken to, to remind them of their responsibilities; and to an awkward boy in his teens who gazed around the church with unaccustomed and bored eyes. He was unable to understand why he had to be there in the first place still dressed up in his Sunday shorts and grey flannel shirt.

Lionel, delayed, swept in with his white surplice blowing around him as if he were standing out to sea like a tea clipper.

"Baptism is not," he began without a hitch to his arrival though he had to make room for the pressing needs of the wife and husband who felt they should be closer to the vicar and the font than anyone else, "to be regarded merely as a ceremony devised for the Christian naming of inf-"

His eyes had strayed to the font where he was about to operate. It was always a nuisance when someone or other asked for the real thing, being the ancient stone font rather than a brass imitation. This was because it did not have a plug hole so all of the remaining water had to be laboriously bailed and sponged out. The idea of bailing out reinforced the notion the vicar was sailing out to sea but now with a Force Eight storm close by.

"Naming of infants-" he repeated. "Oh good heavens, there's no water."

Ten pairs of eyes strained towards him with considerable curiosity. How would the vicar deal with this small crisis bearing in mind there was no water supply to the church?

At the Far East end a vase of lilies spread itself like a flowering chestnut tree in autumn carefully arranged by the particular lady of the day on the flower roster, a work of art in itself and just right for the small congregation. Without further word, Lionel set sail down to the nave to the altar and snatched the flowers from the vase laying them thereafter in some disarray on the sparkling altar cloth. He then retrieved the vase and its, by now, precious contents. The water, somewhat cloudy was duly emptied into the stone font in his left hand while his right hand held the order of service. His eyes did not stray from the words as he did so judging the pouring by the weight of the glass vase.

"Well now, where were we?" He demanded of his audience. They were unsure and waited patiently while Lionel took hold of the child.

The devil's door had been blocked up for centuries but perhaps, thought the vicar, at that moment there had been just a smidgen of an imp in the nave to cause him grief. If there was, then it would remain for another day as he had nowhere to go. Perhaps the door should be reopened one day? Lionel ploughed on with the well-worn words which alighted on the gathering as if they had been sweetmeats at a Turkish bazaar.

The child cried dutifully though it might have been the rather unpleasant odour emanating from the water rather than the chilling effect of the sprinkling from a height but, nonetheless, another Walton product joined the ranks of the faithful.

*　*　*　*　*

"Well! Just look at this Lizzie. What a change." It was her friend Nancy, arms clenched around a wicker shopping basket.

"Lumme, lawks," said Lizzie in a somewhat profound statement as she stared up as on entering the shop as if it was a cathedral. In fact, the ceiling was only four feet above her diminutive hat pin but the alterations within the shop were so startling it seemed the right thing to say.

"Old Thorley only sold bread and milk-"

"And yeast, don't forget the yeast."

"Not a lot else," chortled Nancy feeling as if she had been let loose in Aladdin's cave, "but, there's everything here you could possibly want...everything," she emphasized as her eyes glowed in excitement.

"From a pin to an elephant," said Bill walking in behind them. "Look at this lot. Syrup of figs, senna pods, medical paraffin, castor oil," he pinched his nose in wry disgust.

"So, can I help anyone with anything or is this just a mutual admiration tour?" asked Mrs Keighley.

"Two Woodbines and two matches please," said Bill tearing his eyes away from the tins of corned beef. He loved corned beef sandwiches especially with Branston pickle. Two large rounds of that out in the fields at lunch and a bottle of bitter, nothing better in the whole world he had been often heard to say.

"Sixpence, please." She turned to her husband who was counting a new pile of postage stamps behind the counter. "Looks like we are going to get rich pretty soon."

The ladies chortled in mirth as their heads bobbed towards each other in a long practised secret ritual before wandering off to the green grocery department. Mrs Keighley was by now banging the top of a packet of dark sugar before deftly folding the blue paper over. "Those carrots Nancy, are really sweet."

Her husband raised his head from counting. "Television's here...in the village ready for the Coronation."

"Who can afford the likes of that I wonder?" queried Lizzie. "I saw one in Leeds. It was turned on in a shop window. Looked like it was snowing heavily but it was a sunny day where ever it was."

"Well, I expect it will get better, as time goes by."

"I like my wireless. I'm never without it. Morning vicar: have you got one of these television thingies yet?"

Lionel was somewhat taken aback by the directness of the query thrown at him. "Morning Ladies, morning Bill. I won't have time for one of those."

"But," said Bill, a man who understood the vicar better than most, "I'm told there will be horse racing in the afternoons."

Lionel's eyes gleamed for a moment. "I might make some enquiries. I assume they are dreadfully expensive?"

"Fourteen inch Bush is about sixty-five guineas," said the font of all village knowledge behind the counter.

"Hmm. I could feed myself for a very long time on that amount of money."

But the ladies could see he was hooked on the idea, as firmly as a pike on a gaff out of the river Wharfe. Lionel himself felt it politic to remain fairly neutral on the subject. If he was to buy a television set before the Coronation, any publicity on the subject would mean that the vicarage in Thorp Arch would be full to overflowing. The idea of a pint of bitter being spilt down his neck as the farming brigade leaned forward to gain a better view in the darkened room tended to dampen his enthusiasm for the new box of tricks, or at least until after the big day.

As he raised his hat to leave, the butcher boy almost collided with him as he cycled off the raised pavement and into the shop before swinging his leg down firmly on the floor.

"Oops, sorry Vicar. Have to get the bacon here by half past."

"Well, be careful," said Lionel crossly, "Old Mrs Jenkins is coming up the path and she can't get out of the way in a hurry as I can."

The lad touched his forelock in a time-honoured fashion and ran into the back of the shop with a side of bacon. Outside, Lionel could see that the gypsies were back in the village. Having officiated at two funerals of their elders in the past where they now rested in the churchyard, Walton had been adopted by the travellers as a stop-off point in their wanderings. He had an affinity with Romany's not shared by many other residents. Like them he shared a passion for horses and would often nod an acquaintance when he was at one race course or another and exchange a few words as they queued at one or another of the turf accountants.

A column of three curved roofed caravans all painted green were proceeding up the road before turning right into Goosemoor Lane. Their horses were well fed on roadside grass and were cleaner than their children who sat up front with their fathers in deep discussion. It was almost as if they had not noticed they were in the village so absorbed in other matters were they which was not matched by a number of women who held onto their children and shot flinty glances onto the road.

Lionel walked back up to the church with his tin of Zebo seeing the animosity in the eyes of his parishioners who were in the road. It wasn't as if the troubles in Cyprus and the *Mau Mau* weren't enough to keep his congregation occupied and they had to remember the gypsies had lost thousands in the German camps not ten years earlier. Theme for a sermon he mused?

*   *   *   *   *

It had been a good evening. The company had been convivial as usual with some excellent port. The meal itself had been far above the average for a Yorkshire village still harassed with the effects of Ted Heath's emergency powers when lights and machinery had been routinely turned off.

Lionel stood in the doorway of the vicarage savouring the night air. He could see one or two stars attempting to break through the cloud cover with a promise of good weather with the dawn. Ideas for a new sermon were beginning to form as they always did at the extreme edges of his consciousness, nudging as if they were trout being tickled in the shallows of a river.

He closed the door and walked back in the hall as a feeling of extraordinary tiredness swept over him. Too much port, he felt, as he sat down in a chair still in the hall.

He could see a bright light in front of him and for a moment he imagined he could hear the long lost choir of St. Peter's joining him in his favourite hymn.

There was a soft rush of air and a gentle sigh from the roof of the house.

*   *   *   *   *

They found him still sitting in his chair, quite dead and undisturbed.

"What a way to go," clichéd one church warden. "We've lost a great character."

"And the ladies of Thorp Arch will miss him too," replied the other as they stood aside for the coffin to be removed from the house. "But, while we bury him we need to think of the future. We need a new vicar."

"It won't be that easy, will it?" said the first, rubbing the side of his nose in contemplation of what they had to do in the interregnum This sort of change was always unsettling to a small community village and after such a powerful, dominant character, his act would be difficult to follow.

Twenty-six recorded vicars and curates over the centuries, some good, one evil, mostly caring. Walton had certainly benefited from their attentions but, with the upheavals in the church beginning to rear their heads in every benefice in the country it would need a very special man indeed to hold the course.

Chapter Twenty-one

Last of The Line

James Scott pressed upwards on his toes into his characteristic pose and leaned over the three ladies who looked up to his six feet with troubled faces.

"Leave it to me. It is not a problem."

The 'problem' to the good women of Walton was the forthcoming fête. The field where the event was to be staged had had, unfortunately, a herd of cows contained within its hedge for a good week. Forty cows produce, amongst other things, a great deal of manure and none of it in a stable condition. There was so much of it, the ladies moaned, that the colour of the entire field was turning from Irish green to one of sage tinged with boiled spinach.

"The fête will be ruined...and the ladies shoes," one had wailed.

"And the children...running around," ululated another.

"Leave it to me," he repeated. "I'll find another venue, a better one...and one with a view," he added realising there was just such a place below the church where the land was level and in pasture. It was clearly important to get the site arranged as soon as possible in the calendar. All it would take is a quick step up the road to plead for the use of the pasture and, naturally, the grass would have to be cut so the ladies would not have to wear boots.

It was, after all, a day when everyone tried a little bit harder. Men would pull out their Sunday suits with a clean shirt;

the children would be dressed in well-pressed shorts and hair slicked down with Brylcream so their skulls showed through emphasizing the lack of flesh on their bodies. And the women? It would be a day of comparisons: sly glances, sometimes in admiration, sometimes in restrained envy at shoes and hats; hem-lines studied of course, the straightness of nylon seams and whether Mrs Braithwaite's lipstick was, well...too red.

It was all part of the game and if the weather was kind, a day to look forward to in the marked up calendar.

Meanwhile, James was busy on other forms of fund-raising ventures. The problem lay in one of the church's bells, known as 'Luke,' for it was badly cracked beyond repair and could not be rung. He was, however, determined to see all three bells ringing together during his turn at Walton. When asked at the fête, which had turned out successfully on the pasture, why he wanted to bother with having the bell repaired because '...three bells can't give us a tune,' he replied: How about three blind mice?"

It was about three months later he received two pieces of positive news in the same day. The first, from his church wardens was to say that through his own enormous effort the funding of the proposed works was almost in place. The second, borne in a brown envelope was from an innovative company in Cambridgeshire. It turned out the company was interested in repairing the cracked bell using a new technique which they had pioneered. There was now a welding process capable of closing the gap in the bronze.

"What have we to lose?" he asked at the next Parochial Church meeting. "The bell is never going to ring again unless we can repair it and we cannot afford to buy a new one."

"But, it is massive vicar, the crack that is, and as for its weight, well-"

"When they were put up there John, they did not have our modern engineering knowledge nor our powerful lifting equipment. We need a scaffold and the louvers on the south face of the tower need to be removed, that's all."

It was simplifying the whole business, he knew, but he wanted those bells to be reunited with its parish.

"But," persisted the other, "it has to go to Cambridge."

"Oh, I'll take it there, and bring it back," he added hastily seeing the inevitable retort forming on the man's lips. "Leave it to me."

At that, the Council members capitulated for they had a vicar here quite determined to see his church restored and that that renovation would include the bells.

Eventually, the great bell was lowered carefully onto the back of a borrowed vehicle at which time James drove it down the Great North Road to Cambridge where the process of intense heat on the bronze brought the bell back into one piece. From there its travels took it on to Loughborough where the world famous John Taylor's Bell Foundry ground the edges to a fine pitch.

It was a great day for the village when the bells pealed out over the green hill each note settling upon the roofs of the houses in Main Street and out beyond to the ancient fields where farmers smiled to themselves at the rightness of it all.

The vicar stopped on his way home to Fairfax House, his temporary house with his family, immensely cheered by his efforts. What ever happened in the future, the bells would be heard and remind his congregation of their connection with the church.

*   *   *   *   *

James Scott had settled into the village as a hand inside a tailored glove. The much vaunted fears in the village that Lionel would be a hard act to follow had not only not materialised but had been improved upon. He was, quite literally, an instant success as his wife and children quickly became absorbed within the fabric of life in the Yorkshire neighbourhood. The church, in its wisdom had purchased a house on the main road, aptly named Fairfax House, so that the vicar would at last be living within his own community, for, although Willie Thomas had lived in what was described as the Old Vicarage next to the church his impact on the parishioners had not been a great success.

James had a mission, a mission to ease the burden of life where ever he could find it with his cry of 'leave it to me,' a regular exhortation during discussion. For James knew, as York knew, that probably the most traumatic events in centuries for the Anglican Church were looming just over the horizon. Like the smoke smudges first seen on that Atlantic skyline when the Bismarck was sighted twenty miles away, Walton was soon to be engaged in its own battle, not of its making, and not one it could ever win. It seemed so unfair.

He was sitting down at his desk one day considering the options open to him when he received the sad news of the death of a much respected and admired farmer in the village. The man had had to fight off considerable worries during his lifetime but had, with his own great personal strengths risen above the troubles and won back what he had lost. His wife, a strong woman who had stood by her man all of the while came to discuss the service which was to be held in St. Peter's.

"We'll need all the space we can get," she said.

James agreed. "Some will just have to stand outside. I hope it doesn't rain, but we can keep the south door open so they can hear the hymns."

"Well, that brings me to the point vicar. I'd very much like to have Amazing Grace played. It was his favourite hymn. Antony, Antony Langford, that is, the organist in Leeds has said he will come and play our organ if it is permissible to you."

James knew the old church would never have another opportunity such as hearing the organ played by such an eminent organist. Dr. Antony Langford was a very well-known recitalist from Leeds and for him to have agreed to play would underwrite the importance of the occasion. The church roof would warm itself on his notes and help guide a new soul to its release.

"We would be delighted," he replied quickly and so it was agreed.

Came the day and the great player from Leeds arrived to be given the order of service and to see what he was to play. He noticed it included a piece called Amazing Grace. Accustomed as he was to playing without music sheets, so familiar were the pieces of church music he was asked to perform, this was a new one to him. He pursed his lips in some dismay for the sheets were now printed and most had been distributed.

"Vicar, I'm afraid I don't know this one."

James Scott opened his mouth in surprise. "Surely everyone knows this hymn, certainly a master of church music?"

"Well, no actually. I'm sorry but I do not recall ever having heard it."

"Umm," said James looking at his watch well aware there was only twenty minutes before the hearse arrived. Already, the church was full as villagers realised they would have to find a seat early on if they were not to stand outside.

"Tell you what," replied the good Doctor quite unperturbed. "You hum it to me and I will write the notes down and together the problem will be quickly overcome."

James smiled. Used as he was to singing and even leading in church this was a slightly taller order but, needs must so he chuckled before beginning to hum the familiar refrain. There, in the vestry the notes of Amazing Grace appeared as if by magic on a sheet of paper. "And there are the words," added the vicar quite sure by now he had been aided by a far greater power than he.

And, as promised, and beautifully played, with the organ humming in delight at its own prowess the hymn was played out to the packed congregation. By the second verse even a minor error had been removed while the mourners had no idea of the minor crisis which had played out in the wings. In fact, the quality of the playing helped lift the singing to a rousing crescendo reminding some standing in the nave of an earlier time when George Thomas, Archdeacon of York had preached in the same pulpit. Grasping the lectern in both hands and smiling down on the vicar's wife whose soprano voice was way above the average, he declared: "By 'eck, you can't half sing in Walton."

As the throng drifted off slowly to drinks in the farmhouse, James Scott returned to the issues on his mind of such importance he needed a clear head and quiet to focus in on the right decisions. He was, by his own villager's comments, 'a quiet man' but 'growing the village' and he was well aware of the tight bonds of the church and the village. He was also conscious, however, of the public's growing need for more transparency and openness in the church and a wish to move with the times. Many were now prepared to challenge the edicts from the Synods not least of whom was the BBC and their searching documentaries. With a loss of a million members from the church, fewer and fewer clergy to take on the gaps created in the ageing Priesthood, a revolution had already begun. James, loyally, would never call it a revolution but in every respect, the church was changing forever.

In Lincoln and other realistic-minded townships came the growing belief that the old established order had to go if only to survive, and be replaced with something new, something strangely original. The idea was dawning on many a learned head in Lambeth Palace that the inspiration of one church, one vicar could no longer be sustained.

"There simply are not enough Priests to go round...and not enough money" he was told at a meeting in York as though Priests were of the same commodity as, say, umbrellas at a rainy fête, besides which the church had handled its vast investments disastrously in the past few years.

"We cannot sustain the old order."

Like a cancer creeping from town to town, village to village came a new cry:

'United Benefices,' whereby one vicar would command several churches at once. After all, went the argument of the day, in many places in England the combined congregations of say, four or even five parishes would not fill one of the churches. Another phrase jumped into the headlines. 'The Redundant churches programme' whereby churches would be mothballed rather in the same way the Royal Navy was fast treating many of its warships, set aside, cocooned for emergencies. James could see a rainy day coming to his own world when his own church would be released from its binding commitments not yet, perhaps and there was always hope for St. Peter's which had weathered many a great typhoon in the past. It was, however, a problem to occupy his mind like nothing before.

"I'm the last of the line," James came to the conclusion. After centuries of a single methodology, now he, like all of his fellow Priests must bow to the inevitable.

It was going to be a gradual process he was relieved to find, not one declaration from the Synod which would place an all-embracing stricture on the land, but come it would, to Walton and, with its size must join up with its neighbours for better and for worse.

At a meeting of the Parish Council several weeks later he chewed his bottom lip as he considered whether he should let them know of the actions being put slowly into place. He gazed across the table in the Hall seeing Yolande the Chairlady, such an awful phrase he thought, slumbering in her seat as usual, expectant faces elsewhere as they waited for his quiet words of good judgment. It was Yolande in fact who had been the first to invite him to Sunday lunch after he arrived in the village in the wake of Lionel Griffith. She had been the perfect host then seeing that he and his family were properly installed and introduced to all the people who mattered to her at least. Now, she trusted him to engage in these meetings where potholes and street lighting were discussed to allow her to nod off and dream of her beloved donkeys.

He made the decision not to disturb the quiet calm of the meeting wishing in a way that the shop still existed in the Main Street. It had always been the method whereby news travelled as fast as the wireless. The whole village would have known by night fall if he had mentioned the fact at the counter. They were going to merge, to be amalgamated like two companies, for the greater good. But four or five churches: how could churches, often so diverse in their politics and beliefs often fervently held, be joined together under one vicar?

James also knew who the parent church was to be. It would have to be the upstart new girl on the street, St. Mary's in Boston Spa, a town unknown and unmapped until spa water was found in the eighteenth century. St. Mary's had only been built ten years before St. Peter's was refurbished after five hundred and fifty years of existence. It was ironic that the sister church with no traditions to guide its fellow benefices, had been chosen to fly the flag of St. George as an Admiral over his particular appointed fleet.

Perhaps, James scribbled on a pad, searching for words for his sermon, perhaps change would be good? Perhaps the great church had governed for far too long in one direction and that traditions needed to be tempered with new ideas springing from a new, modern thinking clergy born after the war.

He would be though, the last of a long line stretching back seven centuries. It was a disheartening notion of the responsibilities placed on their shoulders as he steered his particular ship to safe harbour in, perhaps, unknown waters and with no charts to guide him. And what of his people who had carried him and his wife to their hearts? Would the already diminishing ties loosen further because he wasn't there to re-do the knots?

A tractor went past the window towing a stack of baled hay, wisps of grass filling the air with its smell of the harvest. It replaced the work of fifty farm labourers. Would that the church find such a force to resolve its own problems.

Chapter Twenty-two
At the End of the Day

The coalman's lorry filled with grimy sacks hooted impatiently as the massive bulk of the green John Deere attempted to navigate a passage through the narrow road. Main Street has never allowed two large hay carts to pass each other with ease as each farmer would declare his horses wouldn't or couldn't back up and the resulting blockage would cause many a loud word.

These days a shiny plinth of chrome and metallic painted cars block out the house elevations, an update of the scene from a hundred years ago. Then, the cottages would have had their doors thrown open and head-shawled women would have sat in the openings, knitting and darning and looking out on a dung-covered road created by their own horse-power pollution of the day. Occasionally their eyes would have strayed towards their charges, grand-children often, but others as well left while their parents worked in the fields.

Now, there is no vicar to walk down Main Street to sort out the argument. No vicar, no choir and the church is locked and mostly silent as the graves which surround it. Once in a regular while, St. Peters doesn't even open its ancient south door on a Sunday, cooling the ardour of its worshippers who must make the choice of attending at Thorp Arch or staying at home.

When services *are* held then the mood can slip back to something the village might have recognised a century earlier. Bill, ringing the bell with his sunburned head from harvesting, almost a tonsure in itself. Doreen and Sue, making the collection standing patiently at the end of the pews as church wardens always do while worshippers, never prepared, fumble for their purses as they attempt to keep their places in the hymn book. And Jennifer, there is always a Jennifer, who will add that extra special reason for attending the service, standing by the main door as she distributes hymn books and prayer sheets.

But, the vicar is not there. Only a representative of his church slotted into a roster with four others. And the choir is departed for other shores leaving their stalls empty and hushed causing an uncertain start to the beginning of each hymn as the congregation tunes in as best they can, for the organist is hidden behind his screen unable to lead the way. Below the congregation's feet in the cold glacial clay from that same terminal moraine, the Fairfax's slumber on; how many attending know their well shod feet rest upon the graves of men who led armies and marched with Kings?

Nevertheless, why *should* this be? Villages in England are separated by three to five miles; the convenient distance shank's pony would cover to work or to market. Each village, proud and independent strove to build its own church just as Jethro and Robert had done seven hundred years earlier. The old, the lame, the pregnant mother, young children would all have been able to attend services the more easily by simply walking up the road, congregating in the sun on the path as they waited their turn to enter the south door. And after the services, the vicar who would have known each and every one of his flock as if they were his own family, would be aware of their troubles, their petty foibles and their large peccadilloes, would shake a hand and promise to come visiting '*poor sick Ada*' the next day. This is not to say, of course, it does not happen today, but the vicar two miles away must work such a visit into a very tight programme and be careful that his exhausted mind does not bring him down to the same state as the woman he plans to visit.

Disrobing, this earlier vicar would have strolled down the road towards the Great Hall for Sunday lunch and talk of farming problems, the weather and the seasons and chat about young Willie's find of a new badger set over in the hedge of the six acre.

His place around the table would have been important for he was rated one of the pillars of the village, a man of learning and letters, erudite and capable of making wise decisions on a whole range of subjects in addition to those expected on ecclesiastical matters.

Now, walking up Main Street from Forge House - the old Smithy - to Mrs Jewitt's Post Office - long gone, a visitor will gain a view of the churchyard, grass neatly cut around its stone foundations which thrust out over its northern bank. It looks like a castle in many ways, solid stone ramparts and a view across the countryside towards any invading army. But on enquiry, he or she would find the venerable old building is locked, closed until Sunday unless a special request to open up is made.

Sometimes, an effort is made for St. Peters to be available at certain fixed times in the week much like a museum would be. And, isn't this the case? Isn't Walton church a museum already? Non-worshippers, with their hands clasped behind their backs as if they were visiting Royalty, gaze in silent awe at Fairfax's broken effigy. And others, more local, seek their daughters' wedding, walking proudly down the short aisle, dragging their feet to make the experience last longer, with the chancel bedecked in flowers. Two years later those same people will insist their new-born child be christened in the five hundred year old font despite there being no plug hole, with smiles all round and a vicar borrowed like a cup of sugar, from across the river.

Why does this have to be so? The very fabric of our village life is almost gone. It teeters on the edge of an abyss, the seasons lost with Walton half-empty during the day as the commuters flock to Leeds and York and Harrogate: the 'Golden Triangle' they call it, some with a certain amount of pride in their voice that they can demonstrate their status in life to others. With houses often valued at half a million pounds today, that is the equivalent of five annual poll taxes in the entire country in A.D.1377. There is, thus, a huge gulf between what would be nice and the actuality of the day.

One of the strong threads which holds Walton together is the location of its two main farms one at either end of the parish which act like book ends propping up the church in the middle. It prevents the building from slipping down into the redundant churches programme by the support they bring to the village. Each year, the harvest festival supper is served in the village hall, the same hall that Miss Smith received all of those accolades from the school inspectors a hundred and fifty years earlier.(I wonder what Ofsted would think of that today?).

The scene is timeless with children running between the tables; the sheen on the faces of the women serving up chicken in wine or shepherds pies; the Vicar from Boston Spa engaging in necessary conversation as he re-establishes himself with his flock; Clive on the bar, serving Chardonnay rather than cider and strong beer. Above, in the tie-beams hangs the noise of the residents as they cheer the results of the raffle with a sudden display of a pink or yellow ticket, and all just so they can repair the roof of the tower. Nothing changes does it?

So all is not lost, allowing some of the traditions to remain clinging comfortably like yellow lichen to the stonework and fabric of the village. It is only after the throng has left, saying goodnight noisily to each other, that Walton reverts to its normal life until the next fête in the summer some six months away.

I repeat: why is this so? With every Christian family owning one if not two cars should not Lambeth Palace close two out of every three churches in the country? Aunt Ada and dear old George could be conveyed in comfort and speed to the church which manages to win the lottery to remain open. Births, marriages and burials could continue in those villages which have closed doors at any other time, by special licence: what is, after all, one more piece of paper, one more pink form in this bureaucratic world?

It is always easy to write down ideas, just as those village elders did in such excitement in A.D.1348. And, just as those men scraped together the money to build their own church, are we prepared simply to let the building become moth-balled as if it was a Type 42 frigate at the end of its life? What possible use is such a mausoleum if we were to walk past its oak gates raised to celebrate a great man of the village, knowing there was access only on production of a signed document?

The dilemma surely, lies in the hands of the hundreds of Parochial Church Councils. Technically, all they have to do is arrange porterage each Sunday for Ada and George to the allocated place of worship. It is an attractive thought to many of those clerics across on the south bank of the Thames. It would allow a 'proper' vicar for each property, be-robed and patiently waiting for his larger congregation to arrive. A substantial choir, if there is such a term, one at least that fills the stalls with cheeky faces rising above their snowy white choir robes; an organist who has had time to practice with them on a Wednesday evening so *'everyone sings off the same hymn sheet'*. Their voices will rise as one to the rafters as it had always done in the past. The vicar too, can learn who is sick or anxious and with his own car deliver himself to the door of the needy person the following day. There would be no need for rotas causing the available clergy to split themselves in two with stressed apologies for being late, glancing furtively at the clock on the wall to ensure there is no overrun.

Take out the church and what is left in the village?

The cricket still continues on the other side of the graveyard, down the hill and across the flawless lawns of the present incumbent of the Old Vicarage. Is it not an irony that Walton now has a delightful stone built building fit for a vicar and his family at a time when St. Peters does not have a curate let alone a pastor?

The shop has gone where all the world gossiped while engaged in buying a pound of sugar. It would have been packed and neatly folded for you in blue sugar paper (I use it now for pastel artwork) tamped down on the polished mahogany counter and handed over where you would have been sitting on a bentwood chair, basket on lap with your hat brim at a rather rakish angle.

Let us imagine some interested local determined to open such a store again: where you could find anything you wanted provided you were prepared to wait while he or she shuffled about below the counter in a search of a packet of clothes pegs.

"I know I've got it some somewhere."

A village store has such a comforting, warm feeling about it but would anyone use it to the extent that it would pay? Not far by car, is a shop that has six thousand food items for sale seven days a week. John at the checkout point provides stamps, and pensions are sent directly by electronic mail direct into your current account. With the wonders of computerisation your revised balance is to hand a micro-second later.

There is still something at the bottom of this sieve. If you turn left off the Wetherby Road you will drive up School Lane and see the old school with its carved stone plaque announcing its inauguration date. It still sits on windy hill blessed often by wonderful sunsets silhouetting the two chimney pots which once warmed the children in their short trousers. Artists meet here every week loaded down like Wharfe river fishermen with their tools and canvases. Once a year they put on an exhibition of surprising quality when Waltonians eat home-made biscuits and sip instant coffee as they exchange pleasantries and buy cards for Christmas. On other days, pilates lessons echo Miss Smith's desire for all of her children to have their lungs filled with fresh air each morning. Village elders still meet here to argue over the size, depth and number of potholes or the quality of the street lighting and cottage pies, cooked to a fixed recipe (so they all taste the same) are auctioned off after the Harvest supper.

Down the road, off-centre as it might be described today, a Summer Fayre is in progress to allow all who pay the entry fee to sip Prosecco and eat a bowl of strawberries. Raffles raise astounding amounts of money '...for a good cause'. Even further up the road, there might be a 'Hog Roast' and here the village sits on straw bales as they clap their hands to the caller in the *ceilidh*. Hot pig fat runs down the chins of the farmers and in the roof of the byre where it is held there is a slight chuckle from a long-dead ghost.

At the end of the day almost everything has changed but nothing has changed; only the church on the hill remains as it always has, a beacon for travellers, the centre point of a village thriving even as it had in the times when the Domesday Book was chronicled and a place where we are drawn whether we have a religious bone in our body or not.

What is right, what is absolutely right about all of this is that on Sunday, Bill Kilby, a well respected farmer of Walton will enter the church through that same South door and begin to ring the bells as his predecessors did all those years ago.

This is not the end; it is not the beginning of the end, but it is the end of the beginning.

Winston S. Churchill

Appendix

Some of the terms used in this book might have baffled you – they did to me, so here they are with modern translations.

Carucate: a unit of assessment for land based upon how much eight oxen, pulling one plough, could plough in a single annual season. This is about 120 acres. The carucate was divided into eight each being a bovate i.e. one oxen.

Ox-gang: Amount of land ploughed by one ox in one annual season.

Noble: the first English gold coin produced in quantity with a value of 6/8d or one third of a pound sterling.

Toft: an enclosed piece of arable land.

Croft: a small rented farm usually as a 'croft and toft'.

Rod: A standardised perch or 16.5ft.

Palfrey: A type (not a breed) of horse valued as a riding horse.

Perch: A differing scale of length between 18ft, 20ft or twenty-two ft.

Groat: a silver coin worth four old pence.

Cissor: a tailor of which there were several in Walton.

Synal: A reciprocal obligation.

Tim Whisky: a light one-horse carriage built for rapid action. Mediaeval equivalent of a Porsche.

Squint: an oblique opening in the wall of a church to afford a view of the altar otherwise blocked off.

Hunter: a watch with a hinged cover to protect the glass face.

Page 35.   Value today of 3/-4d is about £67.00